Water From The Well

*Refreshment from the Bible to
Revive your Thirsting Soul*

by
Timothy J. E. Cross

AMBASSADOR

BELFAST, NORTHERN IRELAND
GREENVILLE, SOUTH CAROLINA

Water from the Well
© Copyright 2001 Timothy Cross

ISBN 1 84030 104 X

Ambassador Publications
a division of
Ambassador Productions Ltd.
Providence House
Ardenlee Street,
Belfast,
BT6 8QJ
Northern Ireland
www.ambassador-productions.com

Emerald House
427 Wade Hampton Blvd.
Greenville
SC 29609, USA
www.emeraldhouse.com

Contents

Foreword

With joy you will draw water from the wells of salvation
(Isaiah 12:3).

We all know just how vital water is for our life and well being. In Bible days, before our sophisticated, piped water supply, wells played a very important role in regards to supplying the needed water.

Isaiah here uses the well as an illustration of the blessing of salvation. Salvation, like water, has its ultimate source in God. We desperately need it, but we cannot produce it in and of ourselves. We can, however, bring our buckets to the well - we can bring our empty selves to God, and know that blessed filling and refreshment which only He can give. My prayer is that the following messages, all taken from the Bible, will really prove to be 'Water from the Well' to your soul.

The chapters which follow originated as messages over the monthly *Quiet Corner* spot on the *South Wales Talking Magazine*. For over twelve years now, I have had the privilege of teaching the Word of God in this form. When I first began, the thought of having to prepare a message each month seemed an intimidating order, but the Lord has undertaken for me over the years beyond all that I could ask or think. Blessed be His holy Name!

My sincere desire is that God Himself will now take up the chapters which follow, and use them to His glory, to refresh your soul, feed your mind, warm your heart and generally draw you closer to the Saviour Who promised:-

If any one thirst, let him come to Me and drink. He who believes in Me, as the Scripture has said, Out of His heart shall flow rivers of living water (John 7:37,38).

Timothy J. E. Cross
Barry, South Wales

Chapter One

The One Who Lifts Us Up

In Psalm 3:3, King David testified *But Thou, O LORD, art a shield about me, my glory, and the lifter of my head.* Let us think for a moment about that expression referring to God as being *the lifter of my head.*

The Drooping Head

We all have had cause, at some time or other, to hang our heads. A drooping head reflects a heavy heart and a drooping soul. I can well recall an incident which occurred whilst I was on teaching practice. The deputy head had cause to give a particularly naughty child a severe 'telling off' in front of the class I was observing. It was not a pleasant occasion. The child hung his head in humiliation. A drooping head though is not solely the experience of children. At times of disgrace, at times of discouragement, at times of disappointment, during times when we have cause to be downcast, we too will have a drooping head. So what a verse of hope is Psalm 3:3. *But Thou, O LORD, art a shield about me, my glory, and the lifter of my head.* The verse tells us that God is able to restore to us the joy, the honour and the peace and the equilibrium which we once knew. When we know God, and when we have trusted in His Son to be our Saviour, no matter how dark some of our days may seem, there is still hope. There is always light at the end of the tunnel, for God is near. So another Psalm - a Psalm written by a man who really had reached rock bottom - concludes in this way: *O Israel hope in the LORD! For with the LORD there is steadfast love, and with Him is plenteous redemption. And He will redeem Israel from all his iniquities* (Psalm 130:7,8). Then in Psalm 71:20,21, we can read similar sentiments, along with a positive attitude to troubles in these words: *Thou Who hast made me see many sore troubles wilt revive me again; from the depths of the earth Thou wilt bring me up again. Thou wilt increase my honour and comfort me again.*

The Divine Helper

The God of the Bible then, specialises in lifting up the head that is bowed down - be it bowed down with the weight of sorrow, sadness, stress or shame. David knew it. *Thou, O LORD, art a shield about me, my glory, and the lifter of my head.* Notice that when David wrote these words, he was not writing from a position of ease. The context of Psalm 3 is an insurrection against David's kingship - an insurrection which caused David to flee for safety. To complicate and confound matters, this insurrection was led by none other than David's own son, Absalom. David then, just like you and me, knew his difficulties and dangers along with the seemingly twisted up nature of some of God's providences. He no doubt thought at times 'Why does life have to be like this?' But David took his fears to God, and he wrote this third Psalm with its opening confession *O LORD, how many are my foes! Many are rising against me; many are saying of me, there is no help for him in God.* So it was within this context that David still trusted in God, knowing Him as his shield and protection and mighty deliverer - the God Who lifted up his head.

When we scan a thousand years to David's most famous descendant, the Lord Jesus Christ, 'great David's Greater Son', we see that His ministry was also one of lifting up the downcast. The Lord Jesus explained His manifesto by using the words of Isaiah the prophet:-

The Spirit of the Lord is upon Me, because He has anointed Me to preach good news to the poor. He has sent Me to proclaim release to the captives and recovery of sight to the blind, to set at liberty those who are oppressed, to proclaim the acceptable year of the Lord (Luke 4:18,19).

The Gospel records record Jesus' ministry in some detail. He gave help to the helpless and hope to the hopeless. To those bowed down by sin and oppression He gave -and still gives - deliverance, dignity and reason to live again. An example of this is in Luke 13. We read there of a woman who was literally bowed down and could not look up. *For eighteen years; she was bent over and could not fully straighten herself. And when Jesus saw her, He called her and said to her, 'Woman, you are freed from your infirmity.' And He laid His hands upon her, and immediately she was made straight, and she praised God.*

The Delightful Hope

The Lord Jesus is our all-sufficient Saviour. He is able to lift up our head. He is able to straighten out our crooked lives. He is able to make us see the eternal, lasting treasures of heaven. He is able to make us know, enjoy and praise God, now and for ever. Say then, with David: But *Thou, O LORD, art a shield about me, my glory, and the LIFTER OF MY HEAD.*

Chapter Two

Satisfaction

One of the earliest family outings that I can recall going on, was a very exciting visit to the zoo. It made a great impression on a certain young fellow. Monkeys, giraffes, lions, dolphins . . . One poser to which I never received an answer though was this: 'How many stale buns does it take to satisfy an elephant?'

The physiological term which describes this is 'satiation'. Satiation is that agreeable feeling of feeling full - but not too full - after a meal.

The search for satisfaction

On a more serious note though, what of the answer to the question: 'How much does it take to satisfy the human soul?' For surely the search for satisfaction and fulfilment - a satisfaction and fulfilment that is never quite reached - is one of the engines that drives the world around us. 'If only I was richer.' 'If only I was slimmer.' 'If only I had a better job.' 'If only I looked better.' 'If only I was married.' 'If only I could be single again' . . . and we could go on 'ad infinitum.'

The reason for the search

Did you know that the Bible explains this world's restless search for soul satisfaction? The Bible gives a clear diagnosis of this feverish illness. The Bible teaches that if we seek for ultimate satisfaction in anything or anyone other than God Himself, we will always have an inner hunger and emptiness. Listen to God's Own kind rebuke in Isaiah 55:2, when He says:- *Why do you spend your money for that which is not bread, and your labour for that which does not satisfy? Hearken diligently to Me, and eat what is good, and delight yourselves in fatness.*

This all being so, it comes as less of a surprise to learn that soul satisfaction is one of the Bible's ways of picturing salvation. Let us explore this a little further:-

The satisfied soul

In Psalm 63:5,6, David wrote this from personal testimony: *My soul is feasted as with marrow and fat, and my mouth praises Thee with joyful lips, when I think of Thee upon my bed, and meditate on Thee in the watches of the night.* David's well being here is remarkable in that his external circumstances at the time were exceedingly harsh. He had been driven out of Jerusalem into the barren wilderness of Judah. He was thus away from the visible sanctuary on earth. Yet his circumstances did not dent the inner happiness of his soul. He still enjoyed union and communion with God his maker. It proves the old Christian adage that 'Happiness depends on happenings, but joy depends on Jesus.'

In Isaiah 25:6, God made this promise: *On this mountain the LORD of hosts will make for all peoples a feast of fat things, a feast of wine on the lees, of fat things full of marrow, of wine on the lees well refined.* And when we turn to the pages of the New Testament, we see the fulfilment of this blessed promise. This promise - like many others - was wonderfully fulfilled in God's all-sufficient provision for our hungry souls in the Lord Jesus Christ.

The Bread of Life

Jesus once made the assertion: *I am the bread of life; he who comes to Me shall not hunger, and he who believes in Me shall never thirst* (John 6:35). But Jesus then went on to make this most unusual claim: *I am the living bread which came down from heaven; if anyone eats of this bread, he will live for ever; and the bread which I shall give for the life of the world is My flesh* (John 6:51).

Not surprisingly, the Bible records that Jesus' words here stirred up a great controversy. But what exactly did He mean?

Back to Calvary

Jesus here was actually talking about His impending death on the cross, when He literally gave His flesh for the life of the world. There can be no ultimate human satisfaction without a divine salvation; and it was on the cross that Christ procured our salvation. He gave His flesh for our life - for our pardon; for the forgiveness of those sins which impede our fellowship with God. It is Christ's death - and Christ's death alone - which brings reconciliation to the believing soul - to the soul that, as it were, tastes of the bread of Christ and by faith gratefully feeds on God's provision. Christ's sacrifice of Himself for our sins at Calvary really does give us peace with God, and fellowship with Him for time and eternity. It brings soul satisfaction both now and for ever. The blessedly satisfied state of the redeemed in glory is described in this way by the apostle John in his privileged glimpse of glory: *They shall hunger no more, neither thirst any more; the sun shall not strike them, nor any scorching heat. For the Lamb in the midst of the throne will be their shepherd, and He will guide them to streams of living water; and God will wipe away every tear from their eyes* (Revelation 7:16,17).

O Christ in Thee my soul has found
And found in Thee alone
The peace the joy I sought so long
The bliss till now unknown

Now none but Christ can satisfy
None other name for me
There's love and life and lasting joy
Lord Jesus found in Thee.

Chapter Three

A Total Eclipse of the Sun

The Solar Eclipse

On the 11th of August 1999, at precisely 11.11 am, we in the UK experienced a rather dramatic total eclipse of the sun. The dictionary defines such an event as 'an obscuring of the sun when the moon comes between it and the earth.' Such occurrences are, of course, very rare, and hence a great deal of hype preceded and followed that memorable day in August 1999. Being plunged into darkness for a minute or two during daylight hours was certainly an eerie experience, I recall.

The Saviour's Eclipse

The thought of darkness during the day will cause many Christians to think of Calvary. For when Jesus died on the cross, the whole earth was similarly plunged into an uncanny darkness during daylight hours. In fact, it was darkness at midday. Matthew's Gospel records of that epochal time: *Now from the sixth hour there was darkness over the land until the ninth* hour. *And about the ninth hour Jesus cried with a loud voice "Eli, Eli lama sabachthani?" that is "My God, my God, why hast Thou forsaken me?"* (Matthew 27:45,46). Luke likewise records it this way: *It was now about the sixth hour and there was darkness over the whole land until the ninth hour, while the sun's light failed* (Luke 23:44,45). Interestingly, the marginal reference in some versions of the Bible translates that last phrase as *the sun was eclipsed.*

But what does all this mean? Jesus once described Himself as *the light of the world* (John 8:12), yet on the cross he endured the most terrifying darkness. There is an element of mystery and paradox here to be sure - yet this does not mean that we are dealing with the totally unexplainable:-

The Darkness of Divine Judgement

The best interpreter of the Bible is always the Bible itself. In the Bible, darkness most frequently refers and alludes to divine judgement. Let us trace this theme through:-

i. Darkness was one of the divine judgements upon an unrepentant Pharaoh during the time of the Exodus. *There was thick darkness in all the land of Egypt for three days ... but all the people of Israel had light where they dwelt* (Exodus 10:22,23).

ii The prophet Zephaniah also spoke of God's wrath in these terms; *A day of wrath is that day ... a day of darkness and gloom, a day of clouds and thick darkness* (Zephaniah 1:15 cf. Joel 2:2).

iii. Turn to the pages of the New Testament, and perhaps most formidably of all, we read the Lord Jesus's teaching on hell - hell being the ultimate in divine judgement against unrepentant sinners. Hell is described by Jesus as *the outer darkness* (Matthew 8:12) - an eternal darkness away from the light and love of the God Who is light and love.

In Scripture then, darkness is most frequently associated with God's judgement on sin, and this leads us to the heart of the Christian Gospel.

The Darkness of Calvary

Why was there darkness at Calvary? Why was there darkness associated there with the sinless Son of God, Who alone did not deserve to suffer any divine judgement for sin? The answer of the Scriptures is that Christ was suffering divine punishment, not for His own sins, but for the sins of others. *For our sake He made Him to be sin Who knew no sin, so that in Him we might become the righteousness of God* (2 Corinthians 5:21).

At Calvary, Jesus suffered the darkness of hell, so that all who believe in Him may escape that darkness and bask in the light of heaven. He was dying there in our place, as our substitute. Hence the darkness of divine judgement - the judgement due to us.

> Well might the sun in darkness hide
> And shut its glories in
> When Christ the mighty Maker died
> For man, the creature's sin.

Here then we are dealing with the most momentous event. It was the procuring of the salvation of God's people and it was literally cosmic in its effect. The sinless One was made sin. The living Saviour was dying. The light of the world was made to endure the most terrifying darkness. He Who enjoyed eternal fellowship with God the Father in eternity past, was now temporarily separated from Him, so that all who believe in Him may enjoy eternal reconciliation to God the Father. Substitution is the word which encapsulates it all. Christ was experiencing the darkness of hell in our room and stead. *Christ also died for sins once for all, the righteous for the unrighteous, that He might bring us to God* (1 Peter 3:18).

Come to the light!

So do you understand the meaning of Calvary? Those who trust in Christ now will surely bask in the light and glory of heaven then. Those who reject Christ now are equally surely to be consigned to the blackness of hell. Paul reminded the Christians in Ephesus: *once you were darkness, but now you are light in the Lord* (Ephesians 5:8). *He has delivered us from the dominion of darkness* (Colossians 1:13). All Christians are children of light - children of light because of the darkness of Calvary.

> The Holy One did hide His face
> O Christ twas hid from Thee
> Dumb darkness wrapt Thy soul a space
> The darkness due to me
> But now that face of radiant grace
> Shines forth in light on me.

Chapter Four

Great David's Greater Son

Of the many titles of the Lord Jesus Christ, one which is not so well known is that of 'the Son of David'. This title though figures quite prominently in the pages of Scripture. Matthew 21:9 for instance records how the crowd, on what we call 'Palm Sunday', shouted out to Jesus *Hosanna to the Son of David! Blessed is He Who comes in the name of the Lord! Hosanna in the highest,* and not so long before this, in Matthew 20:30, we can read how two blind men cried out to the Lord as He was passing by *Have mercy on us, Son of David!* What then is the significance of this title - 'the Son of David'?

1. The Sovereign Son of God

We note first of all that David was Israel's greatest earthly king. It was king David who united the nation and established Jerusalem as its religious and political capital. The Jewish people looked back on David's time as something of a golden era, and longed for such again. As 'the Son of David' we are reminded that Jesus is a king; in fact, the Bible describes

Him as the *King of kings and Lord of lords* (Revelation 19:16). Jesus is currently enthroned in heaven, seated at the right hand of God. 1 Peter 3:22 tells us that He has *gone into heaven and is at the right hand of God, with angels, authorities and powers subject to Him.* Reverence then belongs to King Jesus, 'great David's Greater Son.'

The *Shorter Catechism* asks the question 'How doth Christ execute the office of a king?' The answers it then gives is this: 'Christ executeth the office of a king in subduing us to Himself, in ruling and defending us and in restraining and conquering all His and our enemies.' Christ is the Son of David. King David had many faults. In contrast, Christ was sinless. David needed his sins forgiven - Christ is the One Who bestows the forgiveness of sins, by His sacrificial death for sinners on Calvary's cross.

2. The Sovereign Son of the Scriptures

Secondly, the title 'Son of David' reveals that the Lord Jesus Christ is the fulfilment of all the Messianic longings of the Jewish people, and the fulfilment of all the promises God made in the Old Testament Scriptures. In 2 Samuel 7:12 ff. for instance, the Lord promises king David *When your days are fulfilled and you lie down with your fathers, I will raise up your offspring after you, who shall come forth from your body, and I will establish His kingdom. He shall build a house for My name, and I will establish the throne of His kingdom for ever.* In the Lord Jesus, this promise was fulfilled. Do you recall how the angel Gabriel said to Mary of Jesus, about a thousand years later *He will be great and will be called the Son of the Most High; and the Lord God will give to Him the throne of His father David; and He will reign over the house of Jacob for ever; and of His kingdom there will be no end.* Then in Jeremiah 23:5, God also promised *Behold the days are coming, says the Lord, when I will raise up for David a righteous branch.* The 'righteous branch' here tells how the Messiah was to be of David's line - part of his family tree. Humanly speaking, Jesus certainly was part of this. Matthew 1:1 records Jesus' genealogy for us: *The book of the genealogy of Jesus Christ, the Son of David, the Son of Abraham.* Romans 1:3 tells us of *the Gospel concerning His Son, Who was descended from David according to the flesh.*

3. The Supremely Sovereign Son of the Scripture

Lastly, we note that the title 'Son of David' reveals Jesus' supremacy. In Revelation 22:16, the risen, ascended, glorified Christ proclaims this: *I am the root and the offspring of David.* We see here then that whilst Jesus is descended from David, paradoxically He also preceded David. He is David's Lord as well as David's Son. Jesus is the root of David because He is the eternal Son of God. He had no beginning. He is the uncreated Creator. Micah 5:2 re-enforces this. It tells how Jesus would be born in Bethlehem, the town of David. It tells how Jesus would be a ruler, but it also says that His *origin is from of old, from ancient days - from everlasting.* Christ, you see, is the eternal Son of God. He is incomparable in His Person, and hence He is incomparable in the salvation which only He can give, by the eternal sacrifice of Himself for the sins of God's people on Calvary's cross.

So what a loaded title is the title the 'Son of David.' It tells us of Jesus' sovereignty. It shows that He is the key to the Scriptures - the Word of God and the God of the Word. It reminds us that there is none like Jesus. He truly is superlative in His being and superlative in His blessing.

> Hail to the Lord's anointed
> Great David's Greater Son!
> Hail in the time appointed
> His reign on earth begun
> He comes to break oppression
> To set the captive free
> To take away transgression
> And rule in equity.

Chapter Five

All Things Are For Our Good
Romans 8:28

Romans 8:28 is a verse to which Bible-believing Christians turn and return again and again. It is especially a verse to cling to when our lives appear to take a distressing turn. The verse reads like this: *We know that in everything God works for good with those who love Him, who are called according to His purpose.*

Who can begin to measure the help, comfort, assurance and re-assurance that this verse alone has brought to the afflicted soul? Let us quote it again: *We know that in everything God works for good with those who love Him, who are called according to His purpose.*

Without any further introduction, notice that this blessed verse contains three divine realities. These are i. God's Special People ii. God's Sovereign Power and iii. God's Sweet Purpose.

1. God's Special People

Romans 8:28 has a caveat. The verse cannot be applied universally to everyone. No. The verse does not say that everything will turn out ultimately well for everyone, but only for God's people, namely *those who love Him, who are called according to His purpose.* This is another way of referring to a Christian believer.

A Christian is one who has a relationship with God - one who is loved by God and one who loves God in return. Naturally, we do not love God, but by God's Own supernatural saving grace, we are given a love for God when He makes us aware that we are objects of His saving love in Jesus Christ. *In this is love, not that we loved God, but that He loved us and sent His Son to be the propitiation for our sins* (1 John 4:10). *We love because He first loved us* (1 John 4:19).

A Christian, then, is one who loves God - albeit imperfectly - and has been *called according to His purpose.* Two verses later Paul reiterates this calling by saying that *those whom (God) predestined He also called.* A Christian has heard the personal call of God - the effectual call of the Gospel of the Lord Jesus Christ. The call of invitation is a gracious one: '*Come to me all who labour and are heavy laden, and I will give you rest* ' (Matthew 11:28).

Note then the special people designated in Romans 8:28. Out of the great mass of fallen humanity, there are yet those who love God and have been called by God to salvation in Christ. The verse however also shows us something of:-

2. God's Sovereign Power

*We know that in **everything*** - no possible exceptions - *God works for good with those who love Him, who are called according to His purpose.*

Here we are assured of God's total and absolute control over all that is, has been and will be. He is in control of all that happens to us! It is good to know. *The Lord our God the Almighty reigns* (Revelation 19:6). There is no such thing as 'chance' or 'fate' or 'good luck' or 'bad luck' in the life of the believer. Even the unforeseen, sudden calamities of our lives have all been foreseen and taken into account by the all-knowing, all-powerful God of the Bible. He has, in the words of the Catechism 'foreordained whatsoever comes to pass.' The little and the large details, the great and the small . . . are all under His sovereign sway. *From Him and through Him and to Him are **all things*** (Romans 11:36). *(He) accomplishes **all things** according to the counsel of His will* (Ephesians 1:11). *Are not two sparrows sold for a penny? And not one of them will fall to the ground without your Father's will* (Matthew 10:29).

Yes, Romans 8:28 reveals a God Who controls all things by His sovereign power, as well as a God Who calls some people to be a special people. It is these people, thirdly, who may be assured of the sweet purpose that God has for their ultimate well being:-

3. God's Sweet Purpose

We know that in everything, God works for **good** *with those who love Him, who are called according to His purpose.*

Is it really true? Can the losses and crosses, the upsets and grief, and the difficulties, the disasters, the defeats, the disappointments, the discouragement and even the devastations of this life really be for the Christian's ultimate blessing? Romans 8:28 answers in the affirmative. God has, in His wisdom and love, the verse says, somehow weaved the darker providences into His good overall plan and purpose that He has for us.

I am aware, of course, that not all of God's providences seem to be for our good at any one particular time. Providence can seem harsh and bitter, painful and perplexing. Yet consider the harshest providence of all - the cross of our Lord Jesus Christ.

Back to the Cross

The cross was surely the harshest providence of all, and from a human perspective, the most wicked act of all time. On the cross, the sinless Son of God actually tasted hell, and drank the bitterest cup of the wrath of God. Yet from this most harsh providence, our eternal salvation was wrought. There is blessing from the Saviour's buffeting, life from His death, pardon from His pains, deliverance by His damnation, salvation from His sorrow and heaven from His hell. Truly then, in the light of Calvary: *We know that in everything God works for good with those who love Him, who are called according to His purpose.*

Romans 8:28 is in the Bible. It is part of the inspired, inerrant Word of God. Oh to live in its light! Let us take comfort and courage from this blessed verse. It exhorts us to trust God at all times. He is too wise to make mistakes, and too loving to be unkind. Seeing the hand of God in everything enables us to leave everything in the hand of God, knowing *that in everything God works for good with those who love Him.*

The following, anonymous poem *The Pattern of Life* is an especially good illustration of the verse we have been considering:-

My life is but a weaving
Between my Lord and me
I cannot chose the colours
He worketh steadily

Ofttimes He weaveth sorrow
And I in foolish pride
Forget He seeth the upper
And I the under side

Not till the loom is silent
And the shuttles cease to fly
Shall God unroll the canvas
And explain the reason why

The dark threads are as needful
In the weaver's skilful hand
As the threads of gold and silver
In the pattern He has planned.

Chapter Six

Why Are We Here?

A friend of our family once made the following tongue in cheek comment: "Cars are nasty, dangerous things which should always be locked safely away in garages." We found it even more funny to learn that he had a sunken bath tub in his garage. This sunken bath enable him to get under his car for maintenance purposes. His car was actually a rather swish sports car. It was highly polished and tuned for sure - but very rarely driven. It resembled something of a toy to tinker with. It did not readily occur to him that cars were made to be driven!

Our chief end

The first question of the Westminster *Shorter Catechism* is this: 'What is the chief end of man?' The answer given to this is this: 'Man's chief end is to glorify God, and to enjoy Him for ever' - or as a more modern version puts it: 'The primary purpose of life is to glorify God and to enjoy Him for ever.'

A life that is lived apart from or out of fellowship with God our maker therefore means that we are failing to realise our chief end. It is small wonder that such a life will seem pointless, fruitless and frustrating. No matter how physically or mentally well tuned such a life is, its chief end is not being realised. It is just like a well tuned and polished car that stays locked up in a garage, never to be driven about. As a car is made to be driven, we are made for fellowship with God. The writer of Ecclesiastes - having had his fill of all the delights of this world, both wholesome and illicit - came to this conclusion : *Fear God, and keep His commandments; for this is the whole duty of man* (Ecclesiastes 12:13). Then there is the Psalmist in Psalm 73:25,26 - a Psalm written by a man who was sorely perplexed and puzzled by the seeming injustices of this world, not to mention his own failing health - who came to the following happy realisation and confession about God: *Whom have I in heaven but Thee? And there is nothing upon earth that I desire besides Thee. My flesh and my heart may fail, but God is the strength of my heart and my portion for ever.*

Happy being sad?

At this point, someone may be asking: Why are so many people seemingly content not to realise their chief end? Why do so many seem to settle for living a life that is half dead, and seeking for satisfaction in the things that do not ultimately satisfy and last? Why are the majority seemingly taken up with the things of earth and time, rather than the things of God and eternity? Centuries ago, Isaiah asked the same question of the people of his day! *Why do you spend your money for that which is not bread and your labour for that which does not satisfy?* (Isaiah 55:2). The Bible's answer is that we are in desperate need of both regeneration and reconciliation.

Regeneration by God

Jesus once made the following statement: *Truly truly, I say to you, unless one is born anew, he cannot see the kingdom of God* (John 3:3). By nature, you see, we are born dead to God and His glory. It is only when we are born again, supernaturally by the Spirit of God, that we discover the true, lasting and eternal joys which God has for us - joys which this world can neither give nor take away. We must be born again! It is a matter of regeneration. It is also, however, a matter of reconciliation:-

Reconciliation to God

By nature, we are alienated from God - cut off from fellowship with Him. Our sin separates us from Him now, and will separate us from Him eternally unless it is forgiven. *Your iniquities have made a separation between you and your God, and your sins have hid His face from you* (Isaiah 59:2). We are naturally alienated from God. The good news of the Christian Gospel however is that it is a Gospel of reconciliation. *In Christ God was reconciling the world to Himself, not counting their trespasses against them* (2 Corinthians 5:19). It was on the cross that God, in Christ, dealt with those sins of ours which ruin our fellowship with and enjoyment of God our maker. The Bible is clear: *Christ also died for sins once for all, the righteous for the unrighteous, that He might bring us to God* (1 Peter 3:18). *We also rejoice in God through our Lord Jesus Christ, through Whom we have now received our reconciliation* (Romans 5:11).

The crucial question

The crucial question is therefore: Are you reconciled to God? Have you trusted Jesus to save you? If you have, you will know what life really is all about. You will be fulfilling the purpose for which you were made. You will not wish to change places with anyone in either this life or the next.

Cars are made for driving. You and I are made for knowing, glorifying and enjoying no less than Almighty God Himself. As Jesus said in John 17:3: *This is eternal life that they know Thee the only true God and Jesus Christ Whom Thou hast sent.*

Chapter Seven

God In Three Persons,
Blessed Trinity!

Holy, holy, holy, Lord God Almighty
Gratefully adoring, our songs shall rise to Thee:
Holy, holy, holy, merciful and mighty,
God in Three Persons, blessed Trinity!

And so goes a verse from a well known Christian hymn. You will have noticed that its last line reads: 'God in Three Persons, blessed Trinity.' The doctrine of the Trinity is a fundamental Christian belief and Christian distinctive. This being said though the word 'Trinity' is not actually found in the Bible, yet it is this word which has been used over the ages to encapsulate the God which the Bible reveals. For truth's sake, it is vital that we know as much about the Trinity as we can, for all false religions and faiths are in some sense a denial of the Trinity. If we are wrong here, we will be wrong everywhere. But what are we talking about when we say that the Bible reveals God to be a Tri-une God?

A Definition of the Trinity

There is, of course, something of a mystery and enigma to God. We should expect the Creator to be way beyond the creature, and the finite to be unable to fully comprehend the Infinite. This is especially so here, for it is above and beyond our logic to say that God is both One and that God is Three - yet this is what the Bible teaches us. The *Shorter Catechism* encapsulates the Bible's teaching as follows:-

Q. Are there more Gods than one?
A. There is but one only, the living and true God.
Q. How many persons are there in the God-head?
A. There are three persons in the God-head; the Father, the Son and the Holy Ghost; and these three are one God, the same in substance, equal in power and glory.

The Revelation of the Trinity

The God of the Bible is revealed as a Tri-une God - three in one and one in three. This is the true God, and the only God that there is. As such He demands our exclusive allegiance and obedience. In the first commandment of the Ten Commandments He commands: *You shall have no other gods before Me* (Exodus 20:3).

Interestingly, the Old Testament 'church' also had creeds and precise confessions of faith. One such is Deuteronomy 6:4 which reads: *Hear, O Israel: The LORD our God is one LORD: and you shall love the LORD your God with all your heart, and with all your soul and with all your might.* The Old Testament leaves us in no doubt as regards God's 'one-ness.' And yet the Old Testament also intimates a plurality of persons in this one God. The opening verse of the Bible, for instance reads *In the beginning God* . . . (Genesis 1:1). The word for God here is 'Elohim.' It is the plural of 'El'. If we then proceed to read on in Genesis 1 we can read of the Spirit of God moving over the face of the waters, as well as God speaking. The New Testament (e.g. John 1:14) reveals that this Word of God became flesh in the Lord Jesus Christ, in the fullness of time. The doctrine of the Trinity is therefore very much latent in the Old Testament.

The clearest view of the Trinity however is found on the pages of the New Testament. Consider the time, for instance, when Jesus was baptised in the river Jordan (Matthew 3:13 ff.). The account tells us about Jesus's baptism, and Jesus is the Son of God, the Second Person of the Trinity.

When He was baptised, the Holy Spirit, the Third Person of the Trinity, descended on Him like a dove, and then, most formidably, the First Person of the Trinity, God the Father, spoke from heaven and said *This is My beloved Son, with Whom I am well pleased* (Matthew 3:17).

The Bible therefore clearly reveals that God is one and that God is three. There is a distinction within the God-head of God the Father, God the Son and God the Holy Spirit, and God the Father is God, God the Son is God and God the Holy Spirit is God - yet there is only one God! So even before the world was made, and even before God revealed Himself to us in the Lord Jesus Christ, there existed a community and fellowship within God Himself. He existed in eternity past in a fellowship of Triune love between Father, Son and Holy Spirit. Some (e.g. Patrick of Ireland) have tried to give illustrations of this, but we will reverently refrain from so doing, for surely God is beyond all illustration and comparison.

The Operation of the Trinity

We will never fully understand, let alone comprehend God. Yet if we are Christians, we know that we are and have been objects of the special favour of the Tri-une God. It is God the Holy Trinity Who has saved us. God the Father chose us for salvation in eternity past. He sent His Son to die on the cross to procure our salvation, and He still sends His Holy Spirit to work in our hearts, convicting us of our sins, and leading us to Christ crucified. Then, in trusting Christ, aided by the Holy Spirit, our sins are forgiven and we are reconciled to the Father. Salvation therefore is tri-une, for the God of the Bible is Tri-une. Each member of the Trinity works in perfect harmony for our eternal well being. The apostle Peter brings this out very well in his first letter. Writing to some Christians who were going through painful suffering, he encouraged them by reminding that, inspite of their trials, they had yet been:-*Chosen and destined by God the Father and sanctified by the Spirit for obedience to Jesus Christ and for sprinkling with His blood* (1 Peter 1:2).

Attempting to explain the Trinity is attempting to explain the inexplicable. Volumes and volumes have been written seeking to plumb the depths of the God-head. We trust though that this short chapter will be of help in clarifying the thinking of some. There is always more of God to discover and learn - and Christians, by the grace of the Tri-une God, will have all eternity to carry on discovering and learning more and more of the depths of God's grace, mercy and glory.

There can be no better way of ending this chapter on the Tri-une God by quoting the well known Christian benediction which brings most public worship services to a close: *The grace of the Lord Jesus Christ and the love of God and the fellowship of the Holy Spirit be with you all. Amen* (2 Corinthians 13:14).

Holy, holy, holy! Lord God Almighty
All Thy works shall praise Thy name, in earth, and sky and sea
Holy, holy, holy! merciful and mighty
God in Three Persons, blessed Trinity!

Chapter Eight

Jesus of Nazareth: The Nazareth of Jesus

For some of us, childhood memories are very precious, and revisiting our childhood haunts is a very positive experience, bringing back the carefree days, before the traumas of leaving home, and the minefield of earning our own living.

Jesus' home town

In the Galilee region of Israel lies the town of Nazareth, and it was in this town that the Lord Jesus Christ, the Son of God, was raised, spending both His childhood and early manhood there. Surprisingly, there is no mention at all of Nazareth in the Old Testament Scriptures. It is very doubtful whether we would have heard of this, humanly speaking, obscure town at all if it were not for its blessed association with the Saviour of the world. Jesus put Nazareth for ever on the map! And *He went and dwelt in a city called Nazareth, that what was spoken by the prophets might be fulfilled, 'He shall be called a Nazarene'* (Matthew 2:23). It is noteworthy that

Nazareth is associated even with the risen, glorified Christ - not just His time on earth. In Acts 22:8, we can read how the risen Christ appeared to Paul , speaking these words: *I am Jesus of **Nazareth** Whom you are persecuting . . .*

Jesus' hidden years

The Bible is largely silent about Jesus' so called 'hidden years' in Nazareth - those years before He began His public ministry when He reached His thirtieth birthday. The Bible does however record His being an observant Jew, attending the feast of the Passover with His family when He was twelve yeas old. Similarly, in Luke 4:16 we read how *He came to Nazareth where He had been brought up; and He went to the synagogue, as His custom was, on the Sabbath day.* We see from this that Jesus was accustomed to the public worship of God and the public reading of Scripture. In this, the Redeemer sets an example for the redeemed to emulate. We know that Jesus was acquainted intimately with the Scriptures, knowing them by heart, and able to quote the right and relevant Scriptures at just the right time. In this again, the disciples are wise to emulate the Master, and acquaint themselves with what Paul describes as *the sacred writings which are able to instruct you for salvation through faith in Jesus Christ* (2 Timothy 3:15).

Jesus' home

When the Lord Jesus was raised in Nazareth, His circumstances were those of relative poverty. It is surmised that Joseph, Jesus' earthly father, died when Jesus was quite young, for he is not mentioned again after Jesus' birth. 2 Corinthians 8:9 therefore comes to mind: *You know the grace of our Lord Jesus Christ, that though He was rich, yet for your sake He became poor, so that by His poverty you might become rich.*

It is not so well known that Jesus had earthly brothers and sisters but the Bible records that He did. In Mark 6:3 - back in Nazareth - they said of Jesus: *Is not this the carpenter, the son of Mary and brother of James and Joses and Judas and Simon, and are not His sisters here with us?* When we recall that people of Jesus' earthly rank in first century Palestine would have all lived together in one room, we may speculate that Jesus knew well the stresses and strains which family life can bring, along with the give and take and the necessity of 'digging in.'

Jesus' trade

It was in Nazareth that Jesus both learned and plied His earthly trade. By occupation, He was originally a carpenter. *Is not this the carpenter?* . . . (Mark 6:3). Jesus therefore was no stranger to the world of work. He would have had to sweat at his bench, long before the days of electricity and power tools. He knew toil and honest work - not to mention dealing with awkward customers, out to find fault, grumble and belittle. Human nature has not changed! *We have not a high priest Who is unable to sympathise with our weaknesses* . . . (Hebrews 4:15).

A despised town

The town of Nazareth was not well thought of or highly regarded. Its reputation had got into the popular folklore. Nathaniel may have been quoting a proverb when he asked *Can anything good come out of Nazareth?* (John 1:46). Both theologically and geographically, you see, Nazareth was outside the mainstream of Jewish life. Its population contained a mixture of both Jews and Gentiles, and it was close to the main trade routes of the day. As a stopping place fore merchants and traders, it was something of a nest of immorality and vice - not unlike our towns. Yet all of this notwithstanding, this was where the Lord Jesus Christ lived: He lived amongst all the defilement and degradation, and yet He was uncontaminated by it. He was and is a Friend of sinners, most certainly, but in Himself, as the Bible records, He was *holy, blameless, unstained, separated from sinners* (Hebrews 7:26). The sinless Friend of sinners was thus infinitely qualified and suited to offering up Himself as a sinless sacrifice to save sinners, when the time came for Him to do so.

A town which rejected its Own

Nazareth. Did it have happy associations for Jesus? Well maybe not. In John 1:11 we read *He came to His Own home and His Own people received Him not.* Luke 4:29 even records the rejection of Jesus the Nazarene by His fellow Nazarenes, for *they rose up and put Him out of the city, and led Him to the brow of the hill on which their city was built, that they might throw Him down headlong.* Do you find this surprising? It both is and it is not, and we say that because God had many years previously prophesied a Messiah Who would be rejected. He was de*spised and rejected by men* (Isaiah 53:3). Jesus was rejected at Nazareth, and had to face hostility and rejection throughout His earthly ministry. This rejection however reached its culmination at Calvary, for in His death on the cross Jesus was both rejected by men and forsaken by God Himself, so that whoever believes in Him may know and enjoy reconciliation to God and a glorious home in heaven, for all eternity.

Jesus of Nazareth, a Man attested to you by God . . . (Acts 2:22)

I stand amazed in the presence, of Jesus the Nazarene
And wonder how He could love me, a sinner despised unclean
How wonderful, how marvellous, almost too wonderful to be
How wonderful, how marvellous, great is my Saviour's love for me.

Chapter Nine

Taking The Wanting Out Of Waiting

Have you ever had the not very pleasant experience of having all your well-prepared plans dashed to pieces in an instant? For example, you were certain that a specific job was for you - but you didn't even get on the short list. You were looking forward to going on holiday - but you ended up in hospital instead.

There can be times in our lives when all our props and plans are taken away from us very suddenly, and we are left in a state of great incapacity, uncertainty, and, if we will admit it, even anxiety.

The big question is, What can we do when we don't know what to do? What can we do, also, when we are incapable of doing anything? Well the Bible's answer to this is 'Wait!' Or more specifically, 'Wait upon the Lord.'

Isaiah 40:31 reads like this:-

*They who **wait** for the Lord shall renew their strength, they shall mount up with wings like eagles, they shall run and not be weary, they shall walk and not faint.*

But what exactly does the Bible mean when it encourages us to 'Wait on the Lord'? It means, I suggest, at least three things:-

1. Waiting Patiently

First of all, waiting on the Lord means to have patience. The prophet Jeremiah too knew his trials, tribulations, perplexities, problems, disappointments and even devastation. During the lowest point of his life he wrote the book of Lamentations. In Lamentations 3:25,26 he wrote this:-

*The Lord is good to those who **wait** for Him, to the soul that seeks Him. It is good that one should wait quietly for the salvation of the Lord.*

Trials teach us patience. An urban myth tells of the man who prayed "Lord, give me patience. I want it right now!!" We sympathise with him. When our plans differ from the Lord's plans for us, all we can do is submit. We may propose, but He is God, and is therefore at complete liberty to dispose. The sovereign God has His own time-scale, and it may differ from ours. But who are we to grumble and argue with His wisdom and love? Patience. It is a fruit of the Holy Spirit, and yet a virtue not rated very highly in an age of instant gratification. *Be **patient**, therefore, brethren, until the coming of the Lord* (James 5:7). Patience involves submitting to God and trusting Him at all times. An anonymous Christian once wrote

Trust Him - when dark days assail you;
Trust Him - when your faith is small.
Trust Him - when simply to trust Him, is the hardest thing of all.

2. Waiting Faithfully

Secondly, to 'wait on the Lord' means having faith in the Lord as well as having patience. Psalm 130 is a Psalm written by a man who had reached absolute rock bottom. He opens so:-

Out of the depths I cry to Thee, O Lord.

Then in verses 5 and 6 he writes:-

*I **wait** for the Lord, my soul **waits**, and in His Word I hope; my soul **waits** for the Lord more than watchmen for the morning, more than watchmen for the morning.* Notice what he said again: *I **wait** for the Lord, my soul **waits**, and in His Word I hope.* God's Word is nothing less than the revelation of Himself in the Bible. When we read the Bible we are encouraged to have faith in the God Who reveals Himself there, whatever our present circumstances may be.

The Bible reveals that the Lord is gracious and merciful, slow to anger and abounding in steadfast love. The Bible reveals a God Who is infinite in His wisdom, power and love. The Bible reveals that God is sovereign over all things. The Bible reveals a God Who does not change. The Bible reveals a God Who became man and died on a cross to save us from our sins, so that all will be ultimately well with our souls.

The Bible thus encourages us to have faith and to keep trusting in the God and Father of our Lord Jesus Christ. His love will not let us go. It is not enough just to 'have faith', for faith is only as good as its object. Our faith must be firmly anchored in the God of the Bible. 'Faith is only as good as its object. The man in the jungle bows before an idol of stone and trusts it to help him, but he receives no help. If faith is not directed to the right object, it will accomplish nothing.'

Waiting on God then involves patience and complete trust in Him through good and ill. It also, finally, involves expectation.

3. Waiting Expectantly

Psalm 130, the Psalm of the depths, as we have seen, says *I wait for the Lord . . . and in His Word I hope.* Notice though how this Psalm ends. It ends like this:-

O Israel, hope in the Lord! For with the Lord there is steadfast love, and with Him is plenteous redemption. And He will redeem Israel from all his iniquities.

There is therefore both help for the helpless, and hope for the hopeless in the God of the Bible. With Him there is steadfast love. With Him there is plenteous redemption. He is the God Who sets His people free. His grace is more than sufficient for whatever we may face. God is greater than all our problems. What are our impossibilities to omnipotence? Let us then, by His grace, hope in Him and trust in Him at all times. Let us apply and reapply Romans 8:28 to ourselves:-

We know that in everything God works for good with those who love Him, who are called according to His purpose.

Let us cleave to His promises - the dependable promises of a God Who cannot lie. Let us, by His grace, wait patiently, trustingly and expectantly upon Him. He is the God of all hope; He is the God Who raised the Lord Jesus Christ from the dead. God's people need never be lacking in hope!

Thou Who hast made me see many sore troubles wilt revive me again; from the depths of the earth Thou wilt bring me up again. Thou wilt increase my honour and comfort me (Psalm 71:20,21).

God moves in a mysterious way
His wonders to perform
He plants His footsteps in the sea
And rides upon the storm

Judge not the Lord by feeble sense
But trust Him for His grace
Behind a frowning providence
He hides a smiling face

Chapter Ten

Drinking In The Water Of Life

Strange though it may sound, my idea of an ideal day is to spend a whole day reading in the sun, lying on the sands at Barry Island, just a quarter of an hour's walk from where I write. I recall that on the last sunny Bank Holiday, it seemed that I had the whole world for company! It was the first really hot day of the year and I just loved it. I'm told, however, that too much exposure to the sun can cause skin cancer, so perhaps I should curtail my enthusiasm.

Thirst : Our Physical Need

Lying around sunbathing is thirsty work. It pays to bring your own flask and bottle of water. The iced cold drinks stalls on such days always do a roaring trade. Business booms, but the season does not last for ever. I wonder what they do to make a living in the winter?

Thirst : Our Spiritual Need

The one central message of the Bible is the message of salvation – the gospel of salvation for all who trust in Jesus Christ. Salvation is an all embracing word, and it can be explored from many angles, e.g. God's forgiveness, justification, adoption, propitiation, redemption, reconciliation and others. But did you know that one way of describing salvation, according to the Bible, is of having your thirst quenched and satisfied? It is perhaps the easiest way of all of understanding salvation. Imagine a hot day and you have a raging thirst. It's very uncomfortable . . . but someone comes and brings you a large glass of iced lemonade, the swallowing of which gives you instant relief.

Salvation, according to the Bible, is the thirst-quenching provision for the intense spiritual thirst of the human soul. This provision is provided by none less than God Himself, in His Son Jesus Christ, brought to the believer by the Holy Spirit. Listen to the words of Jesus as recorded by John on two separate occasions, one private and the other public:–

Whoever drinks of the water that I shall give him will never thirst; the water that I shall give him will become in him a spring of water welling up to eternal life (John 4:14).

If any one thirst, let him come to me and drink. He who believes in me, as the Scripture has said, Out of his heart shall flow rivers of living water (John 7:37).

Physical and Spiritual Danger

Dehydration, of course, can be fatal. Thirst is an in-built safety mechanism, urging us to drink so that we can maintain our bodily fluid balance. Thirst then, whilst unpleasant, is actually a sign of life – dead bodies don't get thirsty!

It is the same in the spiritual realm. Not everyone has a spiritual thirst. Why? Well the biblical answer is because they are spiritually dead, and there is no hope for them at all apart from God's making them alive by His Holy Spirit. To be spiritually dead and yet unaware of it is far worse, ultimately, than having your thirst mechanism go awry and dying of dehydration unawares. Our chief end, according to the Catechism, is to glorify God and to enjoy Him forever. How miserable therefore and unsatisfying to seek true enjoyment in anything and anyone other than God.

This was why Jesus said *Blessed are those who hunger and thirst for righteousness, for they shall be satisfied* (Matthew 5:6). The Psalmist too was aware of his burning need for God when he wrote *O God, Thou art my God, I seek Thee, my soul thirsts for Thee, my flesh faints for Thee, as in a dry and weary land where no water is* (Psalm 63:1).

Christ : God's Answer to our Need

The Christian Gospel – and the Gospel alone – provides the remedy for your spiritual thirst. The remedy is Jesus Christ Himself, whose death on the cross for our sins restores all who avail themselves of it to the fellowship with God for which we are designed and secretly crave. Salvation is the quenching of spiritual thirst. It is interesting to note that on the cross, as Jesus suffered the penalty for the sins of God's elect, that He uttered the words *I thirst (*John 19:28). These are the profoundest of words, referring to more than just physical thirst. It's a paradox. Jesus, the giver of living water thirsted, so that whoever believes in Him may never thirst, but enjoy God's salvation forever.

Isaiah 12:3 reads *With joy you will draw water from the wells of salvation*, and in John's description of the redeemed in heaven in Revelation 7, we read, amongst other things that there *they shall hunger no more, neither thirst any more; the sun shall not strike them, nor any scorching heat. . . and He will guide them to springs of living water.*

> I heard the voice of Jesus say
> 'Behold, I freely give
> The living water thirsty one
> Stoop down and drink and live.'
> I came to Jesus and I drank
> Of that life-giving stream
> My thirst was quenched, my soul revived
> And now I live in Him.

Chapter Eleven

Manna From Heaven

A well-known hymn, written in Wales, but loved all over the world, contains the lines

> Bread of heaven, bread of heaven
> feed me now and evermore.

Exodus 16 tells us about the literal 'bread of heaven.' It was a food which God provided miraculously for forty years, and it was given to the people of Israel in the desert wilderness, after God had delivered them from slavery in Egypt. *He rained down upon them manna to eat, and gave them the grain of heaven* (Psalm 78:24).

Exodus 15:15 records that *When the people of Israel saw it,* (i.e. the manna) *they said to one another What is it?* Interestingly, the Hebrew word 'What is it?' is 'Mah hu' - translated 'manna'. This manna was God's gracious provision for His people in the barren wilderness. It was a necessity to keep them all alive, yet it was also very agreeable too. Exodus 16:31

tells us that it was *like coriander seed, white, and the taste of it was like wafers made with honey.*

The manna from heaven. It provided physical sustenance, and it also provides us with spiritual instruction, as we shall now see.

> Day by day the manna fell
> Oh to learn this lesson well
> Still by constant mercy fed
> Give us Lord our daily bread
> 'Day by day' the promise reads
> Daily strength for daily needs
> Cast foreboding fear away
> Take the manna of today

1. Our Total Dependence on God

The manna in the wilderness tells us of our total dependence upon God to meet our physical and spiritual needs. There was nothing in the barren wilderness which would have kept the Israelites alive. The provision of the manna was not a natural provision but a supernatural one. It was from heaven, not from earth. In Deuteronomy 8:3 Moses reminded the people of Israel that *(God) humbled you and let you hunger and fed you with manna . . . that He might make you know that man does not live by bread alone but by everything that proceeds out of the mouth of God.* Jesus encouraged us to pray to God *Give us this day our daily bread* (Matthew 6:11). Every meal that we eat is God's good and gracious answer to our prayers. Giving thanks before we eat is therefore a practice to be encouraged - it enhances our meal times.

2. Our Daily Dependence on God

The manna teaches us of our daily dependence upon God. God instructed the Israelites to *gather a day's portion every day* (Exodus 16:4) enjoining *Let no man leave any of it till the morning* (Exodus 16:19). Some disobeyed the order, and wanted to hoard the manna for future consumption by gathering more than one day's supply. The Bible tells us though that this hoarded manna *bred worms and become foul* (Exodus 16:20) - forcing those who did it to trust God just one day at a time. It reminds us of Jesus' words: *Do not be anxious about tomorrow, for tomorrow will be anxious for itself. Let the day's own trouble be sufficient for the day* (Matthew 6:34).

3. Our Obedience to God

The miraculous manna - provided in a miraculous manner - teaches us lessons in obedience to God's commandments. God provided no miraculous bread from heaven on the Sabbath Day. Yet the narrative records how on the day before the Sabbath, He provided a double portion of manna, and when the Israelites stored it for the Sabbath, it did not go bad. God still commands us to keep the Sabbath Day - now on the first day of the week - holy. The double portion of manna shows that with His commandments He gives the enablements to keep His commandments. It always pays to follow the Maker's instructions.

4. Our Need to use Common Sense: When the Manna Ceased

The manna also provides us with lessons in common sense. The Israelites enjoyed the manna for forty years, right up until the time that *they came to the border of the land of Canaan.* But once in Canaan, we read *the manna ceased . . . they ate of the produce of the land . . . they had manna no more but ate of the fruit of the land of Canaan* (Joshua 5:12).

There was no need of miraculous manna in Canaan, for Canaan was a very fertile land - *a good and broad land, a land flowing with milk and honey* (Exodus 3:8). If the Israelites worked, the land would surely yield its fruit. It reminds us that, normally, God provides for us through the use of means. We pray for daily bread - but we also go out and earn the money to buy it. It is surely presumptuous to expect God to bless our laziness, and provide for us miraculously when it is within our own power to act.

5. The Lord Jesus Christ: The True Bread from Heaven

Finally, the manna is a picture of the Lord Jesus Christ - God's ultimate spiritual provision from heaven for our need. It is Jesus alone Who gives us spiritual life, and it is Jesus alone Who sustains our spiritual life. Jesus once said to the Jewish people of His day - people well-versed in Old Testament history - *I am the bread of life. Your fathers ate the manna in the wilderness and they died . . . I am the living bread which came down from heaven; it any one eats of this bread, he will live for ever* (John 6:48-51).

The question therefore is, Have you tasted of this particular heavenly manna?

Thou art the bread of life, O Lord to me
Thy holy Word the truth that saveth me
Give me to eat and live, with Thee above
Teach me to love Thy truth
For Thou art love.

Chapter Twelve

All About Eve - The Mother Of Us All

To confess all, when it comes to women - 'the fair gender' - I am something of a total ignoramus! I am, of course, very willing to be enlightened, but time and time again, the ways and wiles of women have caught me out and 'weighed me in the balance and found me wanting.' I would like to be able to blame it all on my upbringing in a predominantly male orientated household.

At the risk of being somewhat audacious then, I have entitled this chapter 'All about Eve.' I have done so, as I should like us to consider Eve, the first ever woman. Using the Bible as our guide, we will notice the Making, Marriage, Marring and Marvel of the first ever woman and mother.

1. The Making of Eve

In Genesis 2:18 we read *Then the LORD God said It is not good that the man should be alone, I will make him a helper fit for him.* Genesis 2:21 then goes on to explain how God made woman out of man. Eve was formed out of Adam, for *The LORD God caused a deep sleep to fall upon the man, and while he slept took one of the ribs and closed up its place with flesh; and the rib which the LORD God had taken from the man He made into a woman . . .*

The making of Eve here is most instructive. A famous commentator wrote:-

> The woman was made of a rib out of the side of Adam; not made out of his head to rule over him, nor out of his feet to be trampled upon by him, but out of his side to be equal with him, under his arm to be protected, and near his heart to be beloved.

As the bride of Adam though, Eve is also a type of the Church, for the Church is described in the New Testament as 'the bride of Christ.' Christ, in the Bible, is described as 'the last Adam.' Just as Adam was put into a deep sleep to form Eve, so Christ was put to death to form the Church. Just as Adam's side was pierced when Eve was made, so also Christ's side was also pierced when He hung on the Cross to redeem His Church (see John 19). Interestingly, the Hebrew verb used of God's making of Eve is the verb 'to build.' God *built* Eve from Adam's rib. In Matthew 16:18, the Lord Jesus said of His bride *I will* **build** *My church, and the powers of death shall not prevail against it.*

2. The Marriage of Eve

In full, Genesis 2:22 reads *and the rib which the LORD God had taken from the man, He made into a woman and* **brought her to the man.** Eve, then, was not entirely a free agent when she came to Adam. Her marriage was the work of God - and this is also the case with the Church of Christ and the individuals which comprise this blessed bride. It is God Himself Who draws us to Christ. Jesus said *No one can come to Me unless the Father Who sent Me draws Him* (John 6:44). Thank God then that He does not leave us to our own devices. He is as active in the application of salvation as He was in its accomplishment. Even today, He still effectually calls sinners to Christ. The *Shorter Catechism* defines effectual calling like this:

> Effectual calling is the work of God's Spirit, whereby, convincing us of our sin and misery, enlightening our minds in the knowledge of Christ and renewing our wills, He doth persuade and enable

us to embrace Jesus Christ, freely offered to us in
the Gospel.

Thirdly, on an unhappier note, we notice:-

3. The Marring of Eve

Sadly, Eve's record is not an unblemished one. It was Eve who disobeyed
God and took of the forbidden fruit and persuaded Adam to do the same. In
doing so, they sinned against God and alienated themselves from the
harmony they had previously enjoyed with their Maker. Their action brought
death upon both themselves and us. Their action certainly affected us, for
we have inherited their sinful nature. By nature, we are inclined to sin. By
nature, we are separated from our Maker and need to be reconciled to Him.
Being separated from God is ultimate misery and the source of all misery.
Eve's record then is marred; as children of Adam and Eve, our record is
marred too. But there is hope. Notice last of all:-

4. The Marvel of Eve

The name 'Eve' means 'Living.' Genesis 3:20 tells us that *The man called
his wife's name Eve, because she was the mother of all living.* How though
could Adam name his wife 'Life' when she was responsible for bringing
physical and spiritual death into the world? The answer is that Adam believed
the promise of God. In Genesis 3:15 God promised a redeemer Who would
one day be born through Eve's descendants. Living in our time, we know
that this promise was most wonderfully fulfilled in the Person of the Lord
Jesus Christ. Galatians 4:4 ff explains: *When the time had fully come, God
sent forth His Son, born of woman, born under the law, to redeem those
who were under the law.*

It is Jesus Who gives us life. He said of Himself: *I came that they
may have life, and have it abundantly* (John 10:10). Romans 6:23 reminds
us that *The free gift of God is eternal life in Christ Jesus our Lord.*

Thank God then for Eve, and thank God for motherhood. But thank
God even more especially for the One Who was ultimately born of Eve.
Thank God for the Lord Jesus. For it is through Jesus that the consequences
of Eve's sin are undone. It is through Jesus that our sins are forgiven and
our fellowship with God is restored. It is through Jesus - and Jesus alone -
that we receive the gift of life - eternal life - fellowship with God on earth
and in heaven, here and hereafter, now and for ever.

Chapter Thirteen

He Knows How Much We Can Take

The railway line near where I live never fails to fascinate. Throughout the day, passenger trains run three times per hour, to various destinations, local and national. In between these, freight trains hurtle back and forth to a local power station. Some of these freight trains are very long indeed. I once counted a train with thirty six large coal trucks attached to it. I noticed that these trucks were full of coal, and I also noticed that each truck had its maximum capacity written on its side. From this maximum capacity sign, we can gather that those with the responsibility know what each truck can carry, and are careful not to exceed the maximum load which is stated.

Turning from trains to people though, what about us? What of the heavy loads that we carry around in this life? What of our past hurts, our present stresses and perplexities and our future anxieties? Do you ever fear that you are approaching your maximum load? Do you even fear that if things carry on as they are, you are in danger of 'toppling off the rails'?

The good, comforting and re-assuring news is that, according to the Bible - and if we truly belong to Jesus - such fears as we have mentioned are groundless; for while whilst we can expect all sorts of troubles in this life, God has yet promised that our troubles will never overwhelm us completely. They will not exceed our maximum capacity. Listen to Paul's words in 1 Corinthians 10:13, and seek to take the welcome promise written there on board:-

No temptation has overtaken you that is not common to man. God is faithful, and He will not let you be tempted beyond your strength, but with the temptation will also provide the way of escape, that you may be able to endure it.

Let us now unpack this verse a little.

1. Troubles come our way

No one, but no one is exempt from suffering, says the apostle. *No temptation* (i.e. hard testing) *has overtaken you that is not common to man.* Whilst every one has troubles though, the Christian has a resource of which the non-Christian knows nothing, for:-

2. God is faithful

God is faithful, states the apostle. By this, he means that God is trustworthy, dependable and totally reliable. He will never fail us nor forsake us, for if we belong to Jesus, He loves us with an everlasting love, that will not let us go. But Paul says more. Paul goes on to explain that:-

3. God is in charge of our personal thermostat

God *will not let you be tempted (tried, tested) beyond your strength,* says our verse. How is this so? It is so because in His infinite wisdom, knowledge and love, God our maker knows our maximum capacity. He knows how much we can take. *For He knows our frame, He remembers that we are dust* (Psalm 103:14). Our physical, psychological and emotional make-up holds no secrets to God. *Before Him no creature is hidden, but all are open and laid bare to the eyes of Him with Whom we have to do* (Hebrews 4:13). He knows the very number of the hairs on our head. He knows us better than we even know ourselves. He thus knows how much we can take, and adjusts the trials He sends our way accordingly. They are not accidental but are from our Father in heaven, to fulfil His great overarching purpose for our eternal blessing and His eternal glory. Job, for one, knew this. Four thousand years or so ago, Job went some severe, if not excruciating suffering. Yet through his pains, he could still affirm of God in Job 23:10: *But He knows the way that I take; and when He has tried me, I shall come forth as gold.* Notice though what our verse says about God's dealings with us in and through our trials:-

4. God is well able to deliver us from our trials

With the temptation, says Paul, God *will provide the way of escape, that you may be able to endure it.* 2 Peter 2:9 tells us *The Lord knows how to rescue the godly from trial.* What an understatement! Of course He does. He is the sovereign, omnipotent God. Biblical and personal testimony rings out with the times when God has intervened and removed our seemingly insurmountable difficulties and insoluble problems. He is able to move mountains. *Ah Lord God! Thou hast made the heavens and the earth by Thy great power and by Thy outstretched arm! NOTHING IS TOO HARD FOR THEE . . .* We can approach God's dealings with us in and through our trials from another angle however, and state also that:-

5. God is well able to sustain us in our trials

Biblical and personal testimony can also tell of the times when God has not lightened the load - but He has seen fit to help us endure the load instead. Note that our verse ends with the words: *that you may be able to endure it.*

God knows our capacity, for sure. But nothing can stop Him from increasing our capacity. Paul himself came to know this. He once prayed that God would deliver him from the disabling pain and weakness that he found himself in. His prayer both was and was not answered. God answered Paul's prayer in His Own way. He did not reduce Paul's load, but He did give Him greater strength to carry it. He promised Paul: *My grace is sufficient for you* (2 Corinthians 12:9). And if Paul's God is our God, we too will be able to testify to the all-sufficiency of God's grace.

In summary

The Bible does not promise us an easy journey, this side of heaven. It does though assure us that God is faithful and that He knows our frame. This being so, He will not stretch us beyond our capacity. He is certainly able to remove our trials, but He is also able to give us grace to cope with our trials, and to keep us safe to the last. The God and Father of our Lord Jesus Christ is a God of saving, sustaining and all-sufficient grace. The Bible tells us that this is so. The hymnwriter said:-

He giveth more grace when the burdens grow greater
He sendeth more strength when the labours increase
To added affliction He addeth His mercy
To multiplied trials, His multiplied peace

His love has no limit, His grace has no measure
His power has no boundary known unto men
For out of His infinite riches in Jesus
He giveth and giveth and giveth again.

Chapter Fourteen

The Death Of A Princess

The death of Diana, Princess of Wales, in a car crash in Paris, in the late summer of 1997, shook the British nation severely. Most of us can still remember what we were doing when we first heard the sad and shocking news. Many of us have never experienced an event before or since to compare with it. The whole country seemed to be united in grief, and seemed to close down during the hours of her funeral. During those memorable times, every one seemed to have an opinion, and commentators took up lines and lines of newspaper columns. Is it possible though to consider the whole event in the light of God's Word, the Bible? Yes it is.

1. God's Sovereignty

The Bible would have us see beyond the events that happen in this life, and the secondary causes which bring them about, and look up to the ultimate cause of all things - God Himself. Romans 11:36 reads *for from Him and through Him and to Him are all things. To Him be glory for ever. Amen.* Then Amos 6:6 - a verse which has to be used carefully for sure -

even goes as far as saying: *Does evil befall a city unless the LORD has done it?* We are thus encouraged to see the invisible hand of God lying behind all events, the devastating ones as well as the agreeable.

2. God's Providence

God's providence includes the number of years we will live on the earth, for it is His divine prerogative to both give and to take away life. Acts 17:26 reminds us: *He made from one every nation of men to live on all the face of the earth, having determined allotted periods and the boundaries of their habitation.* Then in Psalm 139:16, the Psalmist says of God: *Thy eyes beheld my unformed substance; in Thy book were written, every one of them, the days that were formed for me, when as yet there was none of them.*

The day of our birth therefore, as well as the exact day of our death, are both dates already written in the divine diary. He is free to bring about the latter by any way He chooses, be it old age, illness or a seeming tragedy. For from the perspective of the Sovereign Lord of all, there is no such thing as a premature death. Job 1:21 is thus rightly proclaimed at Christian funerals: *The LORD gave, and the LORD has taken away; blessed be the name of the LORD.*

3. Our Mortality

The Bible would have us all be reminded - from Prince to pauper - that not one of us is immortal. Death is an appointment, not an accident. *It is appointed for men to die once . . .* (Hebrews 9:27). Death has been a sad fact of life since Adam's Fall. God told Adam: *In the sweat of your face you shall eat bread till you return to the ground, for out of it you were taken; you are dust and to dust you shall return* (Genesis 3:19). One day, either sooner or later, we will leave literally everything we possess behind: *we brought nothing into the world and it is certain that we cannot take anything out of the world.*

4. The Death of Death

Lastly, and best of all, the Bible assures us that if we belong to Jesus, we need not fear death, for to all who truly belong to Jesus, death is the entrance into eternal life - that is the immediate presence of God, the source of all life and blessedness.

John 11:25,26 are usually the first verses quoted at a Christian funeral. They contain one of the 'I am' sayings of Jesus. Jesus said of Himself: *I am the resurrection and the life; he who believes in Me, though he die, yet shall he live, and whoever lives and believes in Me shall never die.* Many other Scriptures corroborate these words. Romans 6:23 for instance reads: *the wages of sin is death but the free gift of God is eternal life in Christ Jesus our Lord.* Revelation 14:13 is therefore logical when it states *Blessed are the dead who die in the Lord.* Note though the exact qualification here - *in the Lord.* That is, believing in Jesus; cleaving to Jesus; trusting in His death on Calvary's cross to forgive us our sins, reconcile us to God and bring us safely to a glorious home in heaven beyond compare.

Christians may not always live well in this world. The Bible does not promise us earthly health, wealth and prosperity. That being said though, Christians most certainly die well, for every Christian has been saved by the grace of God in Jesus Christ.

The death of Princess Diana was a most unusual time. If good can come out of tragedy though, the good was that it drove many Christians to pray for the nation. In the light of the sudden death of Diana, such prayers often took the form of the plea that, many would be prompted to ponder the brevity of time, the nearness of eternity, a hell to be shunned and a heaven to be gained. Above all else, the prayers asked that the nation would turn back to God, and seek the salvation which only the Lord Jesus Christ can give. While the death of Diana still has its mysteries and intrigues all these years later, the Bible is crystal clear as to the way of salvation. *There is salvation in no one else for there is no other name under heaven given among men by which we must be saved* (Acts 4:12). *Believe in the Lord Jesus, and you will be saved* (Acts 16:31).

> Swift to its close ebbs out life's little day
> Earth's joys grow dim, its glories pass away
> Change and decay in all around I see
> O Thou Who changest not, abide with me.

Chapter Fifteen

I Believe In The Holy Ghost,
The Lord, The Giver of Life, Who Proceedeth
From the Father And The Son ...

Fifty days after Easter Sunday sees a day variously known as Pentecost or Whitsunday. As a boy, I used to look forward to what was known as the 'Whitsun Treat' on the Bank Holiday Monday - usually a trip to the funfair at Barry Island. Now, however, I am just a bit wiser, and know that Pentecost is the time when Christians think especially about the great outpouring of the Holy Spirit on the earth, as related in Acts 2 in the New Testament.

Volumes and volumes have been written on both the Person and the Work of the Holy Spirit of God. One short chapter is just a drop in the ocean - but hopefully it will whet your appetite to find out more.

Who is the Holy Spirit?

The Bible reveals that the Holy Spirit is the Third Person in the Divine Trinity of God the Father, Son and Holy Spirit. Jesus promised His disciples that He would be with them always, even after He had ascended back to heaven. Jesus still promises His followers that He will always be with them, to help and comfort them. How though can Jesus be with every Christian at one time? The answer is: By His Holy Spirit. The Holy Spirit can be thought of as the presence of the Lord Jesus with His people, both as a church and as individuals. How wonderful then to know the personal presence of Jesus with us along life's journey - its ups and downs, its sorrows and joys, its tears and smiles, its excitement and its boredom. This is what Jesus promises every Christian *I will pray the Father, and He will give you another Counsellor, to be with you for ever, even the Spirit of truth . . . I will not leave you desolate (lit. as orphans) ; I will come to you* (John 14:16 - 18).

The Spirit's role in conversion

According to the Bible, except for the Holy Spirit's personal working upon us - secretly in our hearts - we will never become Christians at all. The Bible says that by nature we are spiritually dead (Ephesians 2:1 ff.), and we will remain so, apart from the Holy Spirit's imparting of new, 'spiritual' life into our souls.

Spiritual birth however, just like physical birth, is often a painful process. Jesus said *When He* (i.e. the Holy Spirit) *comes, He will convince* (or convict) *the world concerning sin and righteousness and judgement . . .* (John 16:8). The Spirit of God awakens us to our lost plight. He alarms us. He enables us to realise that we are, to put it bluntly, sinners in the hands of an angry God. And yet the self same Spirit also shows us the remedy for our condition. He enables us to flee to Jesus, and cling to Him for mercy, and receive from Him the full salvation which He wrought on Calvary's cross, when He poured out His blood for the forgiveness of sins. Well does the *Shorter Catechism* define 'Effectual calling' as:

'**The work of God's Spirit**, whereby, convincing us of our sin and misery, enlightening our minds in the knowledge of God and renewing our wills, He doth persuade and enable us to embrace Jesus Christ, freely offered to us in the Gospel.'

Jesus said of the Holy Spirit: *He will glorify Me* (John 16:14). The Holy Spirit therefore never draws attention to Himself, but always points away from Himself to Jesus. Those who go overboard on the Holy Spirit therefore may be majoring on the wrong Person of the God-head . . .

The ultimate Author of the Bible

Did you know that the Holy Spirit is the ultimate Author of the Bible? It is a paradox, but the Bible has only One Author, even though it has many human authors. Ultimately, the Holy Spirit is the sole Author of Scripture.

The Bible's explanation of itself is that Scripture is the product of God's out-breathing on the human authors, causing them to write what God wanted us to know, and write it free from all errors and mistakes. *All Scripture is inspired by God* . . . (2 Timothy 3:16). *No prophecy ever came by the impulse of man, but men moved by the Holy Spirit spoke from God* (2 Peter 1:21).

Where would we be without the Bible? It is God's love letter to lost mankind, telling us of the way of salvation through faith in the crucified Christ. It alone is the Book which tells us how we may glorify and enjoy God, and so fulfil our chief end. Yet, we will never understand the Bible without the aid of its Author. The theologians call this the 'illumination of the Holy Spirit.' Jesus promised: *the Counsellor, the Holy Spirit, Whom the Father will send in My name, He will teach you all things . . . When the Spirit of truth comes, He will guide you into all truth.* (John 14:26, 16:13).

The Holy Spirit makes us more like Jesus

Finally, we note that the Holy Spirit of God gradually makes the Christian more like the Lord Jesus Christ. The Holy Spirit makes us holy. Again, the *Shorter Catechism* reminds us 'Sanctification is the work of God's free grace, whereby we are renewed in the whole man after the image of God, and are enabled more and more to die unto sin and live unto righteousness.' Galatians 5:22 surely gives us a miniature picture of the Lord Jesus Christ when it says *the fruit of the Spirit is love, joy, peace, patience, kindness, goodness, faithfulness, gentleness, self-control.*

We have only just skimmed the surface of the Person and Work of the Holy Spirit of God. How though does what we have considered affect you and me? It depends who we are:-

The non-Christian

If you are not a Christian, you have not got the Holy Spirit of God dwelling in you. You need to ask God that, by His Holy Spirit, He will enlighten you to your need, and enable you to trust in Jesus as your own, personal Saviour.

The Christian

The exhortation to the Christian is this: *Be filled with the Spirit* (Ephesians 5:18). We must ask God to fill us with His Holy Spirit, and to keep on filling us with His Holy Spirit. Then only will we be useful and fruitful in Christian service, and then only will we indeed become more like Jesus, and enabled to share something of His love and loveliness with those around us in this increasingly secular world.

> Come, Holy Spirit, come
> Let Thy bright beams arise
> Dispel the sorrow from our minds
> The darkness from our eyes
>
> Convince us of our sin
> Then lead to Jesus' blood
> And to our wondering view reveal
> The secret love of God
>
> Dwell therefore in our hearts
> Our minds from bondage free
> Then shall we know and praise and love
> The Father, Son and Thee.

Chapter Sixteen

Enoch: A Man Who Walked With God

A well worn joke goes along the lines of 'What did the hypochondriac have written on his grave?' Answer: 'I told you I was ill.'

There is a fascinating programme on the radio currently called 'Brief Lives.' Really, it is the radio equivalent of the newspaper obituary column. In this fifteen minute programme, the lives of famous people - or those thought famous - who have recently died are summarised along with the mark that they are perceived to have made on the world.

Enoch: a lesser known character of the Bible

We would be hard pressed to find a finer epitaph than that of the one belonging to Enoch. There are only a few verses in the Bible concerning Enoch, but the ones that we have written about him tell us that he was a man of unusual sanctity. Enoch's 'obituary' - if indeed we can call it that - is recorded for us in the fifth chapter of the book of Genesis. It reads as follows:-

When Enoch had lived sixty five years, he became the father of Methuselah. Enoch walked with God after the birth of Methuselah three hundred years, and had other sons and daughters . . . Enoch walked with God; and he was not, for God took him (Genesis 5:21,22,24).

What a way to go down in history. *Enoch walked with God* (Genesis 5:24). To 'walk with God' is actually the essence of true religion. This was summarised very well many years after Enoch's time by the Old Testament prophet Micah. In Micah 6:8 we read: *He has showed you, O man, what is good; and what does the LORD require of you, but to do justice and to love kindness, and to walk humbly with your God.*

Whatever we do not know about Enoch, we do know that he was a man who 'walked with God.' By this, we mean that Enoch lived in close harmony and fellowship with God. By this we mean that Enoch acknowledged that God was his maker, preserver and provider, and that he was totally dependent upon God's goodness and mercy every moment of the day. Oh to be an Enoch! Oh to walk with God.

Walking with God through thick and thin

We may think that such a 'walking with God', as we have just mentioned, is not possible for ordinary folks like you and me. We may even be of the view that this 'walk' is only attainable and possible for those who remove themselves from the rough and tumble of life in this world. Wrong! The Bible shows clearly that Enoch was no monastic man. His circumstances were just like ours.

The Bible records that Enoch was a family man. God gave him sons and daughters, with all the blessings that they bring, along with all the stresses and strains they bring as well. We note too that Enoch lived in a world that was no less cruel and callous than ours is today. Enoch was the seventh generation away from Adam. Sin had been in the world for a long time by them. The ground had already been stained by murder (see Genesis 4). Yet in spite of all this, Enoch still maintained close fellowship with God his maker. *Enoch walked with God.*

Remember too that Enoch had no complete Bible, such as we have today. He also lacked any kind of Christian fellowship or the other New Testament means of grace which perhaps we take for granted. Yet Enoch still 'walked with God' and *he was not, for God took him.* i.e. one day, God took Enoch straight away home to heaven. Enoch did not have to go through the process of dying and death. The only other man in the Bible who entered glory in such a way was Elijah - see 2 Kings 2:11. Interestingly, by way of contrast, we note that Adam earlier was never born, but had to taste death, Enoch here was born, but never tasted death, for God took him before he died. Enoch was translated from earth to heaven in an instant. As one commentator has said of Enoch: 'He changed his place but not his company, for he still walked with God, as in earth, so in heaven.'

The inspired commentary

In Hebrews 11:5-6, we can read the New Testament commentary on Old Testament Enoch. It sheds further light upon him, and shows that walking with God and having faith in God are synonymous - they amount to the same thing. *By faith Enoch was taken up so that he should not see death; and he was not found, because God had taken him. Now before he was taken he was attested as having pleased God. And without faith it is impossible to please Him. For whoever would draw near to God must believe that He exists and that He rewards those who seek Him.*

Enoch walked with God: We can walk with God

Enoch walked with God. As such, he is an example for us to emulate - even if at times there is nothing more discouraging than a good example! Enoch's God may be our God, and Enoch's sweet fellowship with God can be ours too, as God actually makes this fellowship possible for us. He has sent His Own dear Son to die on a cross for our sins, to remove for ever the sin barrier between us and our Maker. He has sent His Holy Spirit, the gift of all those trust in Jesus. The Holy Spirit, the third Person of the Trinity, is God's special, personal presence with us day by day, through all the ups and downs and rough and tumble and sorrows and joys of life. He has promised never to leave us or forsake us. By God's grace we too may walk with God. We too, like Enoch of old, may enjoy God's presence with us now, and, by His grace in Jesus Christ, may continue to walk with God for all eternity, as on earth, so in heaven.

Enoch walked with God. Amazingly, so may we.

O for a closer walk with God, a calm and heavenly frame
A light to shine upon the road, that leads me to the Lamb

So shall my walk be close with God, calm and serene my frame
So purer light shall mark the road, that leads me to the Lamb.

Chapter Seventeen

The Best Day Of The Week

I have to confess to having a slight emotional attachment, for various reasons, to Glasgow Rangers Football Club. When the results are broadcast on a winter Saturday, it is good to know how they got on, along with their position - usually near the top, if not on it! - in the league. Rangers, it is quite well known, have the reputation of attracting a fervent 'Protestant' support.

The Christian supporters of Rangers however are highly embarrassed by their increasing practice of playing on a Sunday. Sunday is actually the Christian Sabbath Day, referred to happily in Christian circles as 'the Lord's Day.' Being more engrossed by men kicking a bag of air about than by the things of God, surely says something about the sad spiritual condition of our land. Some folks, it seems, are keener to sing songs on a terrace than they are to sing hymns to God in a place of worship. Of course, soccer has its excitements and attractions, but in the light of eternity - or even at a time of earthly crisis - it will be revealed as somewhat frivolous and trivial.

The day of Resurrection

A true Christian will be anxious to keep Sunday special. The fourth commandment is clear: *Remember the Sabbath Day, to keep it holy* (Exodus 20:8). For the Christian, the first day of the week - Sunday - is the Sabbath Day, for it was on this first day of the week that the Lord Jesus rose from the grave, bringing new life, and new hope to all who believe in Him. Matthew's Gospel records in chapter 28:1 ff. . . . *toward the dawn of the first day of the week, Mary Magdalene and the other Mary went to see the sepulchre . . . the angel said to the women Do not be afraid; for I know that you seek Jesus Who was crucified. He is not here; for He has risen as He said. Come, see the place where He lay . . .*

The change of the Sabbath from the seventh day to the first day is one of the many compelling evidences for the reality of Christ's resurrection. The Jewish Sabbath was a hallowed tradition. It was sacrosanct. It must have taken an awesome, earth shattering event to change the Sabbath Day from one day to another. Such an Event was the resurrection of Christ. Luke records of the early church in Acts 20:7 *On the first day of the week, when we gathered together to break bread, Paul preached . . .* and Sunday has been kept special by Christians ever since - and it always will be, until the blessed Day when Christ returns, and ushers in the eternal Sabbath of righteousness, joy and everlasting peace, in the new heavens and the new earth.

The day of worship

Sports and wholesome entertainment and recreation are good in their place. But on a Sunday, a Christian is occupied and pre-occupied with more important, higher matters. Chief amongst these is the reverent worship of God - the God revealed in the Bible as our Creator and Saviour. Psalm 92 is entitled *A Psalm. A Song for the Sabbath.* Its open lines are *It is good to give thanks to the LORD, to sing praises to Thy Name, O most high. To declare Thy steadfast love in the morning and Thy faithfulness by night.*

A day well spent

On the Sabbath, the Christian will be anxious to hear the Word of God faithfully preached, explained and applied. It is by this means that we become strong in the Faith. In Acts 20:32 we read Paul's words *I commend you to God and to the Word of His grace, which is able to build you up and to give you the inheritance among all those who are sanctified.* On the Sabbath the Christian will enjoy the company of fellow Christians, and both give and receive encouragement to live for Christ and to press on in the Faith in a secular world. On the Sabbath, the Christian will also gather around the Lord's Table, and through partaking of the symbols of the bread and wine, recall the heart of the Christian Faith which is Calvary - the atoning death of Christ on the cross.

The best day of the week

Sunday then is the best day of the week. On it we enjoy a welcome respite from the battles of the week. On it we think more of the things of heaven than the things of earth. On it we receive spiritual fortification for the ups and downs of the week ahead. How careful we have to be that nothing or no one robs us of our Sabbath joy. Good things may rob us of that which is the best. The things of time may rob us of the things of eternity - those solid joys and lasting treasures which none but Zion's children know. God commands us: *Remember the Sabbath Day, to keep it holy.*

The *Westminster Confession of Faith* has this to say about the Christian Sabbath:-

> God . . . in His Word (hath) by a positive, moral and perpetual commandment binding all men in all ages . . particularly appointed one day in seven for a Sabbath, to be kept holy unto Him; which, from the beginning of the world to the resurrection of Christ, was the last day of the week, and from the resurrection of Christ was changed into the first day of the week, which, in Scripture, is called the Lord's Day, and is to be continued to the end of the world as the Christian Sabbath.
>
> This Sabbath is then kept holy unto the Lord, when men, after a due preparing of their hearts and ordering of their common affairs beforehand, do not only observe a holy rest, all the day from their own works, words and thoughts about their worldly employments and recreations, but are also taken up, the whole time in the public and private exercises of His worship and in the duties of necessity and mercy.

For the Christian, Sunday is the best day of the week. It has no peer. *Remember the Sabbath Day, to keep it holy.*

A Sabbath well spent, brings a week of content
And health for the toils of the morrow.
A Sabbath profaned, whate'er may be gained
Is a certain forerunner of sorrow.
(Judge Hale)

Chapter Eighteen

The Death Of Our Beloved Cat

It was a very sad day when Cilla, our beloved family cat, died. She was sixteen years old, very pretty, very affectionate, very friendly and exceedingly talkative. For months afterwards, the house just did not seem the same without her. She was a lovely little black and white cat, with a very big presence.

Is there a Biblical slant on the death of our cat and the sadness that we all feel when we lose one of our pets? I believe that there is:-

1. Our pets are tokens of God's favour

The book of Genesis - and Genesis means 'origins' - reminds us that all animal life owes its origin to God. Genesis 1:24,25 reads: *And God said Let the earth bring forth living creatures according to their kinds: cattle and creeping things and beasts of the earth according to their kinds. And it was so. And God made the beasts of the earth according to their kinds and the cattle according to their kinds, and everything that creeps upon the ground according to its kind. And God saw that it was good.*

The enjoyable company and companionship of our pets is therefore another evidence of the goodness of God our creator to us. Of course, pets are not a necessity. We can live and survive without them. But the generosity of God always gives us more then we deserve, and lifts us way above mere subsistence level. Pets here are comparable with flowers. Again, we can live without flowers, and yet how nice they are to see and smell. Like pets, flowers also enhance our lives and are evidences of God's common grace to us. He is even good to those who never thank Him for His goodness. The Lord Jesus said God *makes His sun rise on the evil and on the good, and sends rain on the just and on the unjust* (Matthew 5:45).

2. Our pets warn us against undue sentimentality

The death of our little cat was a warning to us to guard against undue sentimentality. Biblically, it is bad if we dote on our pets more than we do on people. Animals, you see, according to Genesis, are only creatures. You and I though, according to Genesis, are different. For unlike our pets, we are made in the image of God. Genesis 1:27 says something about us which it does not say about the animals. Genesis 1:27 records: *God created man in His own image, in the image of God He created him, male and female He created them.*

Pets are so nice to have around, and yet pets are not like you and me. Pets cannot have fellowship with God. Pets cannot worship God. Pets cannot pray to God. Pets have a survival instinct, and yet they do not fear death and having to stand before God, the righteous judge of all the earth.

The *Shorter Catechism* opens by asking 'What is the chief end of man?' and it answers it by stating 'Man's chief end is to glorify God and to enjoy Him for ever.' Biologically, it is true that we resemble animals in some, if not many, ways. They sleep, just as we do. They enjoy their food, just as we do. Yet spiritually, we are on a different plane from all animals. We have an immortal soul. We are designed to know God for we are made in the image of God. Sin has defaced the image of God in us for sure. Sin separates us from God, and our sin, unless it is pardoned, will condemn us for an eternity of God's wrath . . .

The Christian Gospel though declares a way - the only way - whereby we can be restored to fellowship with God our maker. It is by simple faith in His Son, the Lord Jesus Christ. The Gospel in a nutshell is John 3:16: *God so loved the world that He gave His only Son, that whoever believes in Him should not perish, but have eternal life.*

3. Our pets remind us of better days to come

The death of our cat - chilling though it was - reminded me that, in God's overall plan, better days are to come. Animals also have a vicious side to them, as well as a loving side. Dogs and cats, for instance, do not mix. Nature is, as we say 'red in tooth and claw.' But according to the Bible, this will not always be so. Better days are to come! One day, the Bible tells us, God will redeem the whole of His creation, and restore it back to its original harmony - the harmony of Eden before the Fall, when Adam had dominion over all the creatures and, more importantly, enjoyed unblemished fellowship with his Maker.

Believers in the Lord Jesus Christ are promised nothing less than redeemed souls, in redeemed bodies, to live on a redeemed earth, for ever. It is almost impossible for us to comprehend at the present moment, with all our difficulties both within us and without. Yet Isaiah 11:6-9 gives us a prophetic glimpse of the coming glorious day when the whole of creation will be redeemed:-

The wolf shall dwell with the lamb, and the leopard shall lie down with the kid, and the calf and the lion and the fatling together, and a little child shall lead them. The cow and the bear shall feed, their young shall lie down together; and the lion shall eat straw like the ox. The sucking child shall play over the hole of the asp, and the weaned child shall put his hand on the adder's den. They shall not hurt or destroy in all my holy mountain; for the earth shall be full of the knowledge of the LORD as the waters cover the sea.

So there is a Biblical slant on the death of my furry friend. God's providence extends to all His creatures and all their actions. In words most reassuring, Jesus taught *Are not two sparrows sold for a penny? And not one of them will fall to the ground without your Father's will. But even the hairs of your head are all numbered. Fear not, therefore; you are of more value than many sparrows* (Matthew 10:29-31).

It is always good to look up, and remind ourselves that God is on the throne, and He *accomplishes all things according to the counsel of His will* (Ephesians 1:11). Losses and crosses come our way, but God promises us His all-sufficient grace (2 Corinthians 12:9). The Lord gives, and the Lord takes away, but blessed be the name of the Lord. Nothing can hinder Him in the fulfilment of His purposes of grace. He will save His people. He will glorify His name. His great, gracious and glorious will can only prevail.

Chapter Nineteen

The Rainbow Of God's Love

Recently, I had the joy of revisiting Belfast in Northern Ireland. Having lived there for many years, it was home from home. The flight from Cardiff Airport to Belfast only takes about fifty minutes, and every time I travel this way, invariably I am treated to the sight of the most beautiful rainbow when I look out of the aircraft window. From the vantage point of an aeroplane, the seven colours of the rainbow form a perfect circle - a circle not evident from the ground. Intrigued, since coming down to earth, I have done a little bit of research and found out this:-

> The rainbow is the prismatic refraction of sunlight as seen as it is reflected upon the clouds during or immediately after a rain shower. Such reflections are seen in concentric circles from an aircraft, but as bows or arcs from the ground (Zondervan Pictorial Encyclopaedia of the Bible).

The beauty of the rainbow has some spiritual lessons for us, if we only have eyes to see. Let us consider four of these now. First of all, a rainbow tells us of:-

1. God's Great Creation

What a master artist and architect is our God. Human artists are able to use colours, but the God of the Bible actually created colour. Rainbows make us gasp. The seven colours of its beautiful arch make us concur with Psalm 19:1: *The heavens are telling the glory of God, and the firmament proclaims His handiwork. Day to day pours forth speech, and night to night declares knowledge.* A rainbow surely gives us some inkling of the beauty, wisdom, immensity and glory of the One Who made it. Secondly, and most famously, from the pages of the Bible, the rainbow also tells us of:-

2. God's Great Covenant

Thousands of years ago, the world was so wicked, that Almighty God saw fit to judge it with a universal flood. The whole world perished, except for one man - Noah - along with his family and select animals. Noah escaped because he obeyed God and built an ark. The ark was Noah's salvation, and his refuge from the wrath of God.

After the flood, God said to Noah: *I establish my covenant with you, that never again shall all flesh be cut off by the waters of a flood, and never again shall there be a flood to destroy the earth* (Genesis 9:11). Then, significantly, Genesis records God saying *This is the sign of the covenant which I make between Me and you and every living creature . . . I set My bow in the cloud and it shall be a sign of the covenant between Me and the earth* (Genesis 9:12,13).

The beautiful rainbow therefore, coming after God's judgement as it did, is a symbol of God's mercy and goodwill towards mankind - it is a sign of His covenant. God's covenant is the binding, unbreakable promise that He makes to bless His people - and God's covenant reached its climax in His Son, the Lord Jesus Christ. The Lord Jesus shed His blood of the New Covenant, so that our sins may be forgiven and we may have peace with God. God promises eternal salvation to all who believe in Jesus.

The rainbow, in Noah's time, came after the judgement of the flood. If we belong to Jesus, we need never fear God's judgement, because on the cross Jesus was judged for our sins, in our place, and has thus exhausted

God's wrath against us. Jesus said prophetically of the time when He would endure the flood of God's judgement at Calvary: *Thy wrath lies heavy upon Me, and Thou dost overwhelm Me with all Thy waves* (Psalm 88:7). The rainbow-promise of Noah's day reminds us of the glorious Gospel promise that There *is therefore now no condemnation for those who are in Christ Jesus* (Romans 8:1). With a little meditation, we can also see, thirdly, that the beautiful rainbow speaks to us of something that we all feel our need of, that is:-

3. God's Great Care

Surprisingly, the rainbow's appearing in the sky is as dependant upon the unpleasant and more foreboding clouds and rain as it is upon the more agreeable rays of the sun. Which one of us doesn't prefer the sun to the rain? Believers though can expect clouds and rain this side of eternity. *Through many tribulations we must enter the kingdom of God* (Acts 14:22). What do we do when the dark, difficult, disappointing and depressing days come our way? Don't we look for the rainbow of God's promise? God says in His Word: *My grace is sufficient for you* (2 Corinthians 12:9). God promises in His Word: *I will never fail you nor forsake you* (Hebrews 13:5).

> Days of darkness still come o'er me
> Sorrow's path I often tread
> But the Saviour still is with me
> By His hand I'm safely led.

Finally, looking ahead, the rainbow also speaks to us of the better days which are surely to come. For the rainbow tells us of:-

4. God's Great Consummation

Did you know that there is a rainbow in heaven? The Apostle John has kindly shared with us his blessed peek into the throne room, with its glorious glimpse of God upon His throne. He noted for us that *round the throne was a rainbow that looked like an emerald*. We noted earlier, that the rainbow is actually a circle - it never ends. In His Word, God assures us *I have loved you with an everlasting love* (Jeremiah 31:3).

In heaven, we will be eternally secure in the circle of God's love - saved and safe for ever, all because of the saving love of God in Jesus

Christ. It is His sacrifice alone that is sufficient to save us, for time and eternity.

So, in summary, we have been considering the beauty of the rainbow. It tells us much about the God Who made it - He certainly is a wonderful creator - as it also reminds us that He is the God of the covenant. It reminds us too of God's constant care for His own, in the rain and the clouds as much as in the sunshine, and it also reminds us of His promise of eternal life, when we put our faith in the Lord Jesus Christ.

How good is the God we adore
Our faithful, unchangeable Friend!
His love is as great as His power
And knows neither measure nor end!

Tis Jesus, the First and the Last
Whose Spirit shall guide us safe home
We'll praise Him for all that is past
And trust Him for all that's to come.

Chapter Twenty

Dare To Be An Andrew!

If you are acquainted with the Gospel records, you will know that Jesus chose twelve disciples - see Mark 6:7 and Luke 6:13. We are not told why Jesus chose twelve disciples, but the consensus is that twelve disciples correspond to the twelve tribes of Israel in the Old Testament - showing that all the promises of God are fulfilled in Christ and that those who belong to Jesus now belong to the spiritual *Israel of God* (Galatians 6:16).

Of the twelve disciples of Jesus, some are better known than others. Peter, for instance, is famous for his preaching and pastoral leadership in the early church. Then there is John, the beloved disciple, whose writings take up many pages of the New Testament. Then there is also Judas Iscariot, the one who became a traitor. Judas Iscariot is an infamous man, well known for all the wrong reasons.

For this chapter, let us consider the disciple Andrew. The New Testament does not really tell us a great deal about Andrew. He comes across as an unassuming man, somewhat overshadowed by his more boisterous brother Peter. Yet, Andrew has much to teach us today. While the information about Andrew is relatively sparse, the New Testament shows him to be a man characterised by conversion, concern and converts:-

1. Andrew's conversion

Andrew, by trade, was originally a fisherman, and in the spiritual sphere, he was something of a follower of John the Baptist. 'Was', though, is the word. John 1:35-37,40 reads that one day *John was standing with two of his disciples; and he looked at Jesus as He walked and said, Behold, the Lamb of God! The two disciples heard him say this and they followed Jesus. . . One of the two who heard John speak, and followed Him, was Andrew, Simon Peter's brother.*

Andrew then, whilst not destined for any earthly greatness, was yet a recipient of the highest blessing of all. He was a converted man. He followed Jesus. He knew Jesus as 'the Lamb of God' - the One Who brings redemption from sin and a new, wonderful life of friendship and fellowship with God. Knowing and getting to know Jesus as he did, Andrew, though small in this life, surely would not have wished to change places with Caesar himself! Andrew was one of Jesus' converts. God's grace drew him to Jesus. He was enabled by grace to follow Jesus. He would never forget that day. 'Oh happy day, when Jesus washed my sins away! . . . He drew me, and I followed on, charmed to confess the voice divine.'

Andrew's conversion though was just the beginning. Notice secondly, that with his conversion went:-

2. Andrew's concern

John's Gospel tells us this of Andrew: *He first found his brother Simon, and said to him We have found the Messiah (which means Christ). He brought him to Jesus* (John 1:41,42). So what a brother was Andrew. He brought his brother, Simon Peter, to Jesus. Andrew had a concern that others should know Jesus too, along with the joy of the salvation that He alone can give. Andrew began 'at home' and brought his brother, Peter, to Jesus.

All this reminds us that the Christian Faith is an evangelistic Faith. It has a concern for the eternal souls of men and women. It seeks to share the Good News. How? Well there are many ways. There is the personal testimony that we may share - how we come to Jesus and how He has transformed our lives. There is a prayerful concern for those we know who are outside of Christ. Then what about a personal invitation to come to a church service - the place where above all else the Gospel is preached? For one of the main tasks of the church is to preach Christ crucified as the only Saviour of sinners. Andrew was blessed with a conversion. His heart also was burdened with a concern for other's spiritual well being. Lastly though, we note:-

3. Andrew's converts

Andrew brought Peter to Jesus, and, unknown to him, Peter was to be used in a spectacular way by God. On the day of Pentecost, for instance, Peter preached and no less than three thousand souls were saved and added to the church (see Acts 2). Yet, humanly speaking, Peter would not have been preaching at all if Andrew had not at first brought him to Jesus and been a part of the salvation chain.

When we think of the influence that Andrew had on Peter, and then Peter's great influence on the three thousand and more, we can see what the Bible means when it likens the Word of God to seed sown on the ground. The Word was sown in Andrew's heart and it brought a great harvest in due time. As Jesus said in His famous 'Parable of the Sower' *As for what was sown on good soil, this is he who hears the word and understands it; he indeed bears fruit, and yields, in one case a hundred fold, in another sixty, and in another thirty* (Matthew 13:23).

Andrew then, one of the less prominent of Jesus' disciples, is a great encouragement for you and me, as we plod along in an unspectacular way, in a limited sphere, in our small corners.

When you are feeling down, think of Andrew. We may be nothing in the eyes of the world, yet we can know the greatest blessing of all - the salvation of God in Jesus Christ. We may be only too aware of our limitations, but can certainly pray and seek to share the salvation we enjoy with others, and who knows just what one of those we bring to Jesus may accomplish in the kingdom of heaven. The message then is DARE TO BE AN ANDREW!

Now to Him Who by the power at work within us is able to do far more abundantly than all that we ask or think (Ephesians 3:20).

Chapter Twenty-One

Protection From The Elements

It is said that we British are notorious for talking about the weather. It may be something to do with our 'temperate climate.' Somewhere like Israel, for example, has very predictable weather. In Israel a regular six months of wet and cold weather is predictably followed by six months of dry and hot weather. Here in the UK though we are never quite sure of just what the weather will have in store for us from week to week. We chuckle when the weather forecaster on the TV ssems to have covered most of the possible variations all at once.

Living near the sea, here on the S. Wales coast, we are never quite sure what weather to expect. Some times of the year - especially in the Spring and Autumn - it is especially precarious. It is as though we have to be equipped for Spring, Summer, Autumn and Winter all at the same time. At such times therefore an umbrella and a raincoat, but also some suntan lotion and a pair of dark glasses may be evidenced in my flat. It pays to be prepared! It is rare in the UK when we do not need some kind of protection from the weather - protection from the elements.

We can apply 'protection from the elements' in a spiritual, as well as a physical way. When we open the Bible, we see that God Himself provides a needed, welcome protection from both harsh earthly elements and from the harshest eternal elements too:-

God's protection from the earthly elements

When the people of Israel wandered in the wilderness for forty years, Exodus 13:21 tells us: *And the LORD went before them by day in a pillar of cloud to lead them along the way, and by night in a pillar of fire to give them light, that they might travel by day and by night.*
How welcome that cloud and fire must have been. The wilderness was like a desert during the day - but the cloud would have taken the edge off the scorching heat. The wilderness would have been very chilly at night - but the fire would have given the people their welcome warmth.
Psalm 57 consists of a prayer which David made. The prayer was born out of great personal distress. In its opening lines, David prays to God: *Be merciful to me, O God, be merciful to me, for in Thee my soul takes refuge; in the shadow of Thy wings I will take refuge, till the storms of destruction pass by.* When the storms of life were upon David then, he took refuge in God. It begs the question: How do we cope with the elements? What do we do when we are at rock bottom, and at our wit's end? The Bible encourages us to call on God, when trouble calls on us. God says *Call upon Me in the day of trouble* (Psalm 50:15). When we do, it will be our joy to have the same testimony of Isaiah 25:4, where through personal experience, Isaiah was able to praise God with the words: *Thou hast been a stronghold to the poor, a stronghold to the needy in his distress, a shelter from the storm and a shade from the heat.*

God's protection from the eternal elements

Turning from the earthly to the eternal elements, we see that according to the Bible, the most fearful terror of all is that of the wrath of God. It is this terror which will fall with full force on sinners on the Judgement Day. As we are all sinners, how absolutely crucial it is that we obey the Biblical injunction and *flee from the wrath to come* (Luke 3:7). But to where do we flee? The Bible's answer is crystal clear. We flee to Jesus, for it is Jesus alone *Who delivers us from the wrath to come* (1 Thessalonians 1:10).
The death of Jesus on the cross, says the Bible, was a propitiation. *He is the propitiation for our sins* (1 John 2:2). Propitiation is one of the

technical words of the Christian Faith from which we cannot get away. To propitiate means to appease, or to turn aside someone's anger or to pacify. On the cross therefore, Christ took our sins upon Himself, along with God's righteous anger upon them. He died as our propitiatory substitute, that is, He paid the just penalty which our sins deserve, delivering us from having to pay that penalty ourselves - saving us from the most fearful reality of all: the wrath of God.

Liberal theologians have always denied the wrath of God. But if we ever doubt the wrath of God, all we have to do, is to consider the cross of Christ. There we see the wrath of God against sin and sinners. Paradoxically, if ever we doubt the mercy of God, all we have to do, is to consider the cross of Christ as well. It is by the blood of Jesus, shed for sinners on the cross, that whoever believes in Jesus receives the forgiveness of sins and deliverance from the wrath to come. Paul, in writing to some Christians at Rome, enforced this point, reminding them and us: *Since therefore we are now justified by His blood, much more shall we be saved by Him from the wrath of God* (Romans 5:9).

Yes, the British climate can have its extremes. Protection from the harsher elements and extremes is vital for our physical comfort. Yes, life itself can be very harsh. How good then to know that we can seek refuge in God Himself, and in His Son, the Lord Jesus Christ. For in Jesus we are assured of both earthly and eternal safety from all the storms and heat, of both this world and the next.

> Beneath the cross of Jesus
> I fain would take my stand
> The shadow of a mighty rock
> Within a weary land
> A home within the wilderness
> A rest upon the way
> From the burning of the noontide heat
> And the burden of the day.

Chapter Twenty-Two

If Only ...

Some of the saddest words that any human being can say is the heartfelt groan "If only." Which one of us though does not have an "If only"? "If only 'x' had not happened to me." "If only 'x' had happened to me." "If only I hadn't done that." "If only I hadn't behaved and reacted in the way I did." "If only I was cleverer . . . richer . . . healthier . . ."

Twice in John 11, some grieving sisters, Martha and Mary, are heard exhaling their 'If onlys.' Their brother, Lazarus, had just died, and so naturally they were very upset and troubled in spirit. In this state of mind, they came up to Jesus and said to Him: *Lord, if you had been here, my brother would not have died* (John 11:21,32).

"Lord, if . . ." This at once gives us a clue to the Christian way of reacting to all and anything that we have cause to regret. We bring them to the Lord. A Christian should not say "If only . . .", but rather, like Martha and Mary *"Lord,* if only."

What a Friend we have in Jesus
All our sins and griefs to bear
What a privilege to carry
Everything to God in prayer.

Reading through John 11, we note that there are four truths concerning the Lord Jesus there which enable us to live and conquer our 'If onlys.' These four truths are Jesus' commitment, companionship, compassion and control.

1. Jesus' commitment to us

Lazarus had died, and Martha and Mary were, quite naturally, stricken with grief. John 11:5 though tells us this important detail: *Now Jesus loved Martha and her sister and Lazarus.* This makes a world of difference. From this we see that troubles and trials, losses and crosses and whatever causes us grief are not, mysteriously, incompatible with the love of God. Before Lazarus had died, his sisters, we read, sent to Jesus the message *Lord, he whom You love is ill* (John 11:3). We therefore walk by faith, and continue to believe in the love of God for us, even when our circumstances dictate feelings and suggestions to the contrary. When Jesus loves someone, His love is no mere sentimental love. Rather, when Jesus loves someone it means that He desires and will achieve their eternal salvation. *Having loved His Own who were in the world, He loved them to the end* (John 13:1). Jesus is committed to His Own in covenant love. Therefore Romans 8:28 is true: *We know that in everything God works for good with those who love Him, who are called according to His purpose.*

2. Jesus' companionship with us

A friend loves at all times and a brother is born for adversity (Proverbs 17:17). Jesus met Martha and Mary in their grief. In doing so, He proved Himself as their true Friend. Adversity soon reveals our true friends. You may think that you have friends, but come a time of ill health or financial hardship or sudden calamity, how many friends have you left then? Where do they all disappear? The Bible though assures us of God's presence with us within and amidst our trials. Jesus met with those grieving sisters. His company and companionship eased their sorrow. Our Lord says in Hebrews 13:6 *I will never fail you nor forsake you.* What a promise for us to claim and cling to.

3. Jesus' compassion for us

John 11:35 contains the shortest verse in the New Testament. You should have no difficulty in memorising John 11:35. It reads *Jesus wept.* That's all. *Jesus wept.* This short verse alone reveals the infinite compassion of Jesus. He hurts for your hurts. He grieves for your griefs. John 11:38 goes on to report *Jesus, deeply moved again. . .* How good it is to know in this cruel and callous world, that Jesus cares and Jesus sympathises. *We have not a high priest Who is unable to sympathise with our weaknesses.*

Lastly, John 11 also assures us - and counters our 'If onlys' - with the reassurance of:-

4. Jesus' sovereign control over us

Lazarus, Martha and Mary's brother, had died. All seemed lost. All seemed out of control. The sisters' feelings apart though, all was actually well. Jesus said in John 11:4: *This illness is not unto death, it is for the glory of God, so that the Son of God may be glorified by means of it.*

The tragedy in Martha and Mary's household, you see, was no accident but an appointment. Our disappointments are His appointments. God had foreordained it all for His glory. Lazarus had actually died prematurely so that Jesus could raise him from death, and so prove the veracity of His stupendous claim: *I am the resurrection and the life; he who believes in Me though he die yet shall he live, and whoever lives and believes in Me shall never die* (John 11:25,26).

The story of the raising of Lazarus shows that God is in total and absolute control of all our tragedies and 'If onlys.' There is always another side to things and a larger, overall picture and perspective. God is in control. He is sovereign in His purposes. He *accomplishes all things according to the counsel of His will* (Ephesians 1:11). He is building His church. He is saving and sanctifying His people, working all things out for their eternal good and His eternal glory.

'If only . . . Take it to the Lord, and dwell much upon His commitment to you, His companionship with you, His compassion for you and His sovereign control over you and all that happens to you.

Leave to God to order all thy ways
And hope in Him whate'er betide
Thou'lt find Him in the evil days
Thy all-sufficient strength and guide
Who trusts in God's unchanging love
Builds on the rock that nought can move.

Chapter Twenty-Three

A Little Bit Of Advice To Tim

In 1 Timothy 5:23, Paul wrote the following personal and practical advice to my namesake Timothy, as Timothy battled against ill health and discouragement, and did his best to pastor a congregation of believers at Ephesus. Said Paul to Timothy: *No longer drink only water, but use a little wine for the sake of your stomach and your frequent ailments.*

Poor Timothy then did not always enjoy the best of health. Specifically, he suffered from stomach pains. I for one can relate to this as such goes in my family. I never knew my paternal grandfather, because he died from stomach trouble before I was born. My father would have died from the same stomach disorder, were it not for advances in surgery. Yours truly has inherited a weakness in this area too, hence every ache and pain 'down below' has me a little rattled.

What though, can we learn from 1 Timothy 5:23? It is not exactly a text that you would hang on your wall: *No longer drink only water, but use a little wine for the sake of your stomach and your frequent ailments.* Before we consider the verse, it would be good if we attempted to approach it with a humble spirit. Some have abused this verse. They have misused it to 'prove' that the Bible teaches either total abstinence or self indulgence - depending on what they want the Bible to teach. This rider apart though, consider the following:-

1. Christians get sick too

The first and obvious point is that Christians are not immune or exempt from suffering illness. Paul obviously had a great affection for Timothy - young Timothy was a fine Christian man - but Timothy's godliness did not remove the matter associated with your *stomach and your frequent ailments.*

There is currently a false, sub-Christian dogma around which preaches that 'health and wealth' are every Christians new-birthright. The Bible gives the lie to this though. 2 Corinthians 12:7 describes an excruciating 'thorn in the flesh' suffered by the apostle Paul. In 2 Timothy 4:20 Paul recalled *Trophimus I left ill at Miletus.* Similarly, in Philippians 2:27 we can read of one *Epaphroditus* who at one time *was ill, near to death.* Thank God then for good health and bodily strength - but do not be unduly surprised if sickness and illness come your way.

2. Christians should be sensible

The Bible encourages us to use sensible means to get better when we are ill. *Use a little wine* wrote Paul to Timothy. Timothy perhaps thought that a minister of the Gospel should be a total abstainer, lest his example led someone else astray. Indeed, in 1 Timothy 3:3 we see that one criterion fitting one to be a church leader was *a bishop (overseer) must be above reproach . . . no drunkard.* Paul though encouraged a medicinal use of wine when writing here to Timothy. This may not seem to be very 'spiritual' - but it was very wise when we consider that the water supply in the Roman Empire was not quite up to our stringent standards.

From this, we note that whilst there is nothing wrong at all with praying for good health and healing, there is also nothing wrong with using the means that God has given us to make us feel better - be it a visit to the doctor, taking a pain relieving paracetemol, being able to share a burden with a concerned friend, or, more drastically, emergency surgery. Even Paul, a great man of prayer, enjoyed and benefited from the medical expertise of *Luke the beloved physician* (Colossians 4:14).

3. God can use us in spite of our handicaps

The verse we are considering - 1 Timothy 5:23 - encourages us because it shows that God does not only call those with robust physical health into His service. It also reveals that even frequent illness need not be detrimental to us spiritually, preventing us from walking the path God has allotted for us.

You may wonder why Paul did not suggest - or even order - young Timothy to give up the Christian ministry altogether, and retire on the grounds of ill health. But he did not. Rather, he exhorted and encouraged him to persevere.

We too are to persevere. The Bible teaches us that God may not see fit to remove illness, weakness and manifold other difficulties from our path. But the Bible does assure us of God's grace to live with, cope with and even overcome whatever handicaps we have. In 2 Corinthians 12:9, when Paul was in agonising pain, God Himself promised him: *My grace is sufficient for you, for My power is made perfect in weakness.*

Our almighty, omnipotent God certainly cannot be limited by us. He will surely fulfil His purpose for us and through us, our handicaps notwithstanding. *The LORD will fulfil His purpose for me* (Psalm 138:8). We just have to trust Him and carry on, doing what we can, where we are, with the limited talents and tasks He has given us. Do do you remember the time when Jesus fed five thousand, using such a meagre resource as one young boy's packed lunch?

4. Christians will enjoy perfect health in God's time

Finally, be assured that, if you are a Christian, one day you will enjoy perfect health. The full-orbed Christian hope is not just the salvation of the soul but also *the redemption of our bodies* (Romans 8:23). When Christ returns to the earth, the Bible promises us that He *will change our lowly body to be like His glorious body, by the power which enables Him even to subject all things to Himself* (Philippians 3:21).

One day then we will be forever free from pain. No more 'bad tums for Tim'! Indeed, Isaiah prophesied that in the glorious Age of the world to come: *no inhabitant will say I am sick* (Isaiah 33:24) - for God is going to re-create us and give us glorious resurrection bodies, fitted for the new heavens and the new earth. The prospect is incredible, but Revelation 21:4 says that one day: *God Himself will be with them; He will wipe away every tear from their eyes, and death shall be no more, neither shall there be mourning nor crying nor pain any more, for the former things have passed away.*

Here then was a little bit of advice from Paul to Timothy. *A wise man listens to advice* (Proverbs 12:15).

Chapter Twenty-Four

Happy Birthday To You!

On August 4th 2000, the Queen Mother celebrated her 100th birthday. The celebration was a national one, here in the UK. Reaching a hundred years is a remarkable achievement by all anyone's reckoning - on current form, some of us doubt if we will live to reach half of that age.

Did you know that John Calvin, the French Reformer, once said words to the effect that 'Christians should always celebrate their birthdays in glad remembrance of all God's mercies.' There is nothing in the Bible that commands a birthday party specifically, yet when done in the right spirit, it is surely very much in-line with Biblical thought.

1. Giving thanks for our first birthday

Birthdays remind us that it is in God our maker that we *live and move and have our being* (Acts 17:28), and that *He Himself gives to all men life and breath and everything . . . having determined allotted periods and the boundaries of their habitation* (Acts 17:25,26).

It is God Who made us - He did not ask us for our permission that we should be born. And God has not only made us, but He has also sustained us right up to the present moment. The air that we breathe, the food that we eat, the clothes that we wear and our very existence itself . . . they are all testimony to the goodness and generosity of God. In Acts 14:15 ff., Paul reminded some Pagans - those who did not as yet believe in the true God - that they too were recipients of the bounty of God, even if they did not know it or appreciate it, for the *living God . . . made the heaven and the earth and the sea and all that is in them . . . He did not leave Himself without witness, for He did good and gave you from heaven rains and fruitful seasons, satisfying your hearts with food and gladness.*

Thankfulness is therefore a Biblical imperative. When we count our many blessings, and when we name them one by one, it always will surprise us what the Lord our God has done. Psalm 92 opens so: *It is good to give thanks to the LORD, to sing praises to Thy Name, O Most High; to declare Thy steadfast love in the morning, and Thy faithfulness by night.* A hymn writer wrote the following 'anytime' hymn. It is suitable on a birthday as it is suitable on the other three hundred and sixty five days of the year:-

> Now thank we all our God
> With heart and hands and voices
> Who wondrous things hath done
> In Whom this world rejoices
> Who from our mother's arms
> Hath blessed us on our way
> With countless gifts of love
> And still is ours today.

2. Giving thanks for our second birthday

Secondly though, birthdays are also a reminder that to enjoy the kingdom of heaven, it is not enough to be born, but we have to be born again. We have to be able to recall our spiritual birthday - our second birth - if we are to enter heaven when we die. The Lord Jesus pulled no punches when He told a man who was high up in this world's order: *Truly, truly, I say to you, unless one is born anew, he cannot see the kingdom of God* (John 3:3).

The Bible declares that we are born sinners. *Behold, I was brought forth in iniquity, and in sin did my mother conceive me* (Psalm 51:5). As such, we are unfit for God's presence, and as such, we have to be born anew. The new birth refers to the absolutely radical change which the Holy Spirit effects in us - a change which makes us fit for heaven.

In and of ourselves, we are unable to make ourselves acceptable to God. Yet the Christian Gospel declares that what we cannot do, God in His grace does for us. He bestows on us the second birth. He saves us by His grace in Jesus Christ. He cleanses us from our sins and bestows on us His free gift of eternal life. Note carefully what Paul wrote to Titus in Titus 3:4-7: *but when the goodness and loving kindness of God our Saviour appeared, He saved us, not because of deeds done by us in righteousness, but in virtue of His own mercy, by the washing of regeneration and renewal in the Holy Spirit, which He poured out upon us richly through Jesus Christ our Saviour, so that we might be justified by His grace and become heirs in hope of eternal life.*

Birthdays: A matter of life and death

You must be born anew said the Lord Jesus. We can no more give ourselves spiritual life than we gave ourselves physical life. It all goes to show that salvation is not a natural gift but a super-natural one. It is not by human graft but all by God's grace. The Bible warns us that if we have only been born once, we will have to face *the second death, the lake of fire* (Revelation 20:14). Yet the Bible also reassures us with the glad news that those who have been born twice will most certainly enter into the joy of eternal life in God's everlasting kingdom of light.

The need of the hour then is not reformation but regeneration - new life in Jesus Christ. What about you? Can you celebrate your spiritual birthday? Remember those crucial words of the Lord Jesus: *Unless one is born anew he cannot see the kingdom of God* (John 3:3).

A ruler once came to Jesus by night
To ask Him the way of salvation and light
The Master made answer in words true and plain
'You must be born again'

You children of men, attend to the word
So solemnly uttered by Jesus the Lord
And let not this message to you be in vain
'You must be born again'.

Chapter Twenty-Five

Joseph Of Arimathea: A Major, Minor Character Of The Bible

One of the major, 'minor' characters of the Bible is a man by the name of Joseph, who hailed from the Jewish town of Arimathea. Truth be told, we do not know a great deal about this Joseph - it is as though he walks in and out of the limelight in just a few seconds.

The Holy Spirit Who caused the Bible to be written though, has ensured that a brief paragraph is devoted to Joseph of Arimathea in all four of the Gospel accounts, Matthew, Mark, Luke and John. This shows that the Holy Spirit would have us know about and learn from Joseph - a man described as *a disciple of Jesus, but secretly, for fear of the Jews* (John 19:38).

In a nutshell, Joseph was to make his outstanding mark on world history as the one who provided his own new rock tomb as the place in which the Lord Jesus was buried, after He had been crucified. What then can we learn from what we know of the life of Joseph of Arimathea? At least three things:-

1. Joseph of Arimathea was devoted to the Lord Jesus

Joseph's devotion to the Saviour is very evident from the Gospel records. His greatness then was not intrinsic, but by association with the Son of God. After all the cruel hate of Calvary, Joseph's tender love for Jesus is very moving. Luke, for instance, records how Joseph *went to Pilate and asked for the body of Jesus. Then he took it down (from the cross) and wrapped it in a linen shroud, and laid him in a rock-hewn tomb, where no one had ever yet been laid* (Luke 23:52 ff.). From this we see that Joseph was devoted to the Lord Jesus both in life and in death - and herein lies his greatness. Herein lies our greatest blessing too, for it is in a faith-union with Christ that we - insignificant though we are in the world's eyes - receive God's gift of eternal life. Paul explained to the Romans:- *Do you not know that all of us who have been baptised into Christ were baptised into His death? We were buried therefore with Him by baptism into death, so that as Christ was raised from the dead by the glory of the Father, we too might walk in newness of life. For if we have been united with Him in a death like His, we shall certainly be united with Him in a resurrection like His* (Romans 6:3-5).

2. Joseph did one thing well

Joseph of Arimathea is remembered primarily for just one thing: he was the human provider of Jesus's tomb. He, according to Matthew 27:60 *laid* the body of the Lord *in his own new tomb which he had hewn in the rock.*

At the beginning of His earthly life, God provided the Lord Jesus with a virgin womb; at the end of His earthly life, God provided Jesus with a virgin tomb, and He did so through His servant Joseph.

There is a message for us here and it is this: Put your all at God's disposal, for He can use it in a much greater way than you can ever conceive. The message for us also is to do one thing well for God. Joseph's one thing was his disposal of his tomb for the Lord. Some of us are hindered and handicapped by the knowledge that we are not widely gifted. Yet surely there is at least one thing we can do for the Lord which will bring glory to Him and blessing to others. By God's grace, let us seek out this one matter - a task which is unique to ourselves - and let us do it with all the zeal and strength that God gives us.

3. Joseph's tomb became a vacant tomb

Joseph of Arimathea and the empty tomb of the resurrection morning are inextricably bound. The resurrection of the Lord Jesus Christ is one of the fundamentals of the Christian Faith. Joseph buried Jesus, lovingly and securely, in his own tomb - but three days later Jesus rose from the dead. Joseph's tomb could not contain Him.

The earliest Christian creed - a minimal 'Statement of Faith' explains how *that Christ died for our sins in accordance with the Scriptures, that He was buried, and that He was raised on the third day in accordance with the Scriptures* (1 Corinthians 15:3,4). The detailed fulfilment of Scripture which occurred here is inexplicable apart from Divine inspiration. Hundreds of years previously, Isaiah foretold of Christ *they made His grave with the wicked and with a rich man in His death.* Matthew 27:57 describes Joseph as *a rich man from Arimathea . . .* David wrote in verse 10 of the Messianic Psalm 16: *Thou dost not give me up to Sheol, or let Thy godly One see the pit.* This prophecy was also wonderfully fulfilled on the first Easter morning, when the message of the angel rang out from Joseph of Arimathea's empty tomb: *He is not here; for He has risen as He said. Come see the place where He lay* (Matthew 28:6).

Joseph of Arimathea. He is a major, minor character of the Bible. We do not know a great deal about him, but we do know that He loved the Saviour. He devoted his all to Jesus, and he did one thing well. He did what he could, with what he had, to the glory of God and to the glory of the risen Saviour Who conquered the grave, and is still at work in changing lives, even today.

> He lives triumphant from the grave
> He lives eternally to save
> He lives all glorious in the sky
> He lives exalted there on high
>
> He lives to bless me with His love
> And still He pleads for me above
> He lives to raise me from the grave
> And me eternally to save.

Chapter Twenty-Six

He Made Them High And Lowly, And Ordered Their Estate

On my last visit to the city of Londonderry in N. Ireland, my attention was caught by plaque on a house. On this plaque, words were written to the effect that 'Mrs C. F. Alexander lived here.'

Mrs Alexander was the wife of the Dean of Londonderry, and she lived from 1823 to 1895. Her main claim to fame is that of being a gifted hymn writer, and in this sphere the Church is very much in her debt. Some of her classic hymns include *There is a green hill far away*; *Once in royal David's city* and the favourite children's hymn of praise to God the creator *All things bright and beautiful*.

Did you know that the original version of *All things bright and beautiful* contains a verse which is so controversial, that it has been left out of most modern hymn books? The verse in question goes like this:-

The rich man at his castle
The poor man at his gate
God made them, high and lowly
And ordered their estate

The question is, is this controversial verse right? Can it be proved to be in-line with the teaching of Scripture - our final authority on all matters of Faith? Well unpalatable though it may seem, yes it can. Scripture teaches that ultimately, God Himself is the creator and upholder of all things, and God's providence is the final explanation for why things are as they are. Let us now cite some quotations from the Bible that show that this is indeed so:-

It is likely that Mrs Alexander had Proverbs 22:2 in mind when she wrote this verse. Proverbs 22:2 tells us *The rich and the poor meet together; the LORD is the maker of them all.*

Turning to Revelation 4:11, we glimpse some of the exuberant worship of heaven, which praise God using the words: *Worthy art Thou, our Lord and God, to receive glory and honour and praise, for Thou didst create ALL THINGS, and by THY WILL they existed and were created.* The verse is crystal clear: all things owe their existence to God - animate objects or inanimate objects, animal life or human life. A cat does not decide to be a cat, any more than a man decides to be a man. Then, and we say it sensitively, God makes some male and others female; He gives some robust health, whilst others struggle with handicap and sickness; some are naturally intelligent, whilst others are much slower on the uptake; some are born rich or with the ability to get rich, whilst others spend all their life in poverty. How do we explain all these differences? Well ultimately, God's will is the final and absolute explanation for all things. *Many are the plans in the mind of a man, but it is the purpose of the LORD that will be established* (Proverbs 19:21). God's is the royal prerogative. He is the Governor, and we are the governed. Ephesians 1:11 reminds us that God *accomplishes ALL THINGS according to the counsel of His will.* Romans 11:36 assures us that *from Him and through Him and to Him are ALL THINGS. To Him be glory for ever. Amen.*

I wonder then why Mrs Alexander's verse has been censored so? Is it because it cuts us down to size? It is humbling to human pride for sure, and yet it is surely good to be reminded that God is God, and as God is God, we must let Him be God, for He is God and He will be God! He is 'God most high', the supreme King of kings and Lord of lords. *None can stay His hand or say to Him What doest Thou?* (Daniel 4:35). The *Westminster Confession* has this to say:-

> God, from all eternity, did, by His most wise and holy counsel of His own will, freely, and unchangeably ordained whatsoever comes to pass, yet so, as thereby neither is God the author of sin,

nor is violence offered to the will of the creatures;
nor is the liberty or contingency of second causes
taken away, but rather established.

In closing, what is the value of Mrs Alexander's controversial verse? Much. But I make just three suggestions:-

1. Knowing that God has ordered our estate teaches us to fear and revere Him. God alone is worthy of our praise. He is the Almighty, and we are commanded to worship Him alone. *For the LORD is a great God, and a great King above all gods* (Psalm 95:3).

2. Knowing that God has ordered our estate teaches us to submit to God's will. We are not the captains of our fate or the masters of our souls - God is. We may propose, but God is entitled to dispose, hence *you ought to say 'If the Lord wills, we shall live and we shall do this or that'* (James 4:15).

3. Knowing that God has ordered our estate gives us great comfort. Often, when we look at life from a logical perspective, it seems unfair. I, for one, can relate far more to the poor man at his gate than to the rich man in his castle! On our darker days we may be tempted to say 'What have I done to deserve this?' The theological perspective though sees the hand of God in all things. Sh*all not the Judge of all the earth do right?* (Genesis 18:25). *It is the LORD; let Him do what seems good to Him* (1 Samuel 3:18). *For the LORD of hosts has purposed, and who will annul it? His hand is stretched out and who will turn it back?* (Isaiah 14:27).

The God of the Bible is almighty, absolutely just, infinitely kind and all loving. We know that this is so because of the cross of the Lord Jesus Christ. The cross was the supreme demonstration of God's justice and mercy. So may the good things which seem to elude us, along with the bad things which come our way un-invited, all have the effect of casting us more closely upon our God and His all-sufficient grace.

The rich man at his castle
The poor man at his gate
God made them high and lowly
And ordered their estate

Another hymn teaches the same sentiments, but in a different way. I will end with this:-

Whate'er my God ordains is right
Holy His will abideth
I will be still whate'er He doth
And follow where He guideth
He is my God
Though dark my road
He holds me that I shall not fall
Wherefore to Him I leave it all.

Chapter Twenty-Seven

Those Incredible Christians

Did you know that the designation a 'Christian', whilst in common use today, is rather rare in the Bible - the foundation document and final authority of the Christian Faith? The Bible, in fact, only uses the actual term 'Christian' three times:-

i. *Yet if any one suffers as a **Christian**, let him not be ashamed, but under that name let him glorify God* (1 Peter 4:16).

ii. *And Agrippa said to Paul, 'In a short time you think to make me a **Christian!**'* (Acts 26:28).

iii. *In Antioch the disciples were for the first time called **Christians*** (Acts 11:26).

There then are the only three Biblical references to the term 'Christian' - the more common Biblical designation being words such as a 'disciple', 'believer', 'brother', 'sister', or even the generally misunderstood word: a 'saint'.

The first 'Christians'

You will have noticed that the term a 'Christian' originates from Acts 11:26, in a passage which describes the life of a gathering of Christians in the city of Antioch in Syria. *In Antioch the disciples were for the first time called Christians.*

The term 'Christian' today has perhaps lost something of its value. If someone professes to be a Christian, it is good to ask them what they mean by that, and whether their definition squares with that of the Bible. Not all professors are actual possessors, it has been aptly said. Yet you can be absolutely certain that the Christians in first century, pagan Antioch, were the genuine article.

The Christian Church at Antioch

Antioch was the third largest city in the Roman Empire. Being a member of the Christian community there must have been a thrilling experience - even if being a believer then had its perils and dangers.

The Bible describes the church at Antioch as a mixed, multi-racial community, composed of Jews and Greeks. In this we see the Gospel of reconciliation in action. The Christ whose precious blood reconciles us to the Father, also reconciles us to one another.

Acts also describes the church in Antioch as a preaching centre, specifically: preaching *the Lord Jesus* (Acts 11:20). This is very much in-line with Paul's affirmation that *Faith comes from what is heard and what is heard comes by the preaching of Christ* (Romans 10:17). Similarly, Acts also describes the church in Antioch as a teaching centre. Paul and Barnabbas were the teachers, and wonderful teachers they were too, and well received by a congregation new in the Faith, and eager to learn in the school of Christ. It is small wonder therefore that this church in Antioch had to cope with an agreeable problem of a rapidly growing, expanding congregation: *And the hand of the Lord was with them, and a great number that believed turned to the Lord. . . and a large company was added to the Lord* (Acts 11:21,24).

The Christian community in Antioch - unlike the rather weak and ineffectual community that the church seems to be at times today - made an impact on the society around them. The Christians stood out. They were a beacon of light in a dark word. They attracted attention and scorn, but they could not be ignored. *And in Antioch the disciples were for the first time called Christians* (Acts 11:26).

A blessed nickname

It is most likely that the term 'Christian', as used in Antioch, was originally a nickname, given by the surrounding Gentile world. The word 'Christ' means 'Messiah' or 'anointed one.' A Jew would not use this term so lightly and refer to 'Messiah's people'. A Gentile though, mistaking 'Christ' for a name rather than a title, may well have referred to the church community as 'Christ's ones' - Christians, that is, those who are followers of Christ. Whatever the exact origins of the term, it has become the most commonly used name to designate and describe a follower of Christ now.

In its true sense, the term 'Christian' is a badge of honour like nothing else, for a true Christian really is 'Christ's one' - one who unashamedly belongs to the Lord Jesus Christ, having been united to Him by saving faith.

A Christian

To explore what it truly means to be a Christian would take several volumes. We can state though that if we are a Christian it is because we have been chosen *in Him before the foundation of the world* (Ephesians 1:4). To be a Christian is to know Christ and all the benefits and blessings which only He can bestow. Chief among these is redemption - freedom from the penalty and power of sin. *In Him we have redemption through His blood, the forgiveness of our trespasses, according to the riches of His grace* (Ephesians 1:7).To be a Christian is to enjoy the presence of Christ, day by day, through all the happy and harrowing experiences of this life. To be a Christian is to have hope for the future. Romans 8:17 assures us that if we belong to Christ, we have been adopted into God's family, never to be cast out. As God's very Own children, we are nothing less than *heirs of God and fellow heirs with Christ.* What an inheritance will be ours one day . . .

So, although the original use of the term 'Christian' was a somewhat disparaging term of derision, and although being a Christian, even today, can make us an object of scorn, if we truly belong to Jesus, we will not want to change places with anyone. We are objects of God's special and saving favour in Christ. Our sins are forgiven for His sake. We have been reconciled to our Maker. We are heading for a glorious home in heaven, and in heaven, we shall still be Christians. We shall belong to our blessed Lord and Saviour, Jesus Christ, for all eternity, to the praise of His glory and grace.

In closing, the crucial question is begged: Are you a true Christian? Do you really belong to the Lord Jesus Christ? Can you testify with sincerity:-

> Now I belong to Jesus, and Jesus belongs to me
> Not for the years of time alone, but for eternity.

Chapter Twenty-Eight

The Dawning Of The Light

In Psalm 130:5,6, the Psalmist bares his soul and confesses: *I wait for the LORD, my soul waits, and in His Word I hope; my soul waits for the LORD more than watchmen for the morning, more than watchmen for the morning.*

The watchmen on the walls

In Bible times there was a much greater fear of darkness than today. Cities then lacked the benefits of electricity and the street lighting which we enjoy. Cities in Bible times were fortified by city walls, and these walls would have had watchmen stationed upon them, to alert the inhabitants to any enemy invasion. The watchmen would all have taken their turns, but we can surmise that watching over the city at night would have been the least popular shift. It must have been somewhat creepy. It certainly must have seemed long and tedious. How they must have longed for the morning light, when the darkness would lift, the shadows flee, and they could go home, released from their irksome duty . . . My soul *waits for the*

LORD more than watchmen for the morning, more than watchmen for the morning.

Even though the darkness was real, one thing was equally certain, and that was that dawn would eventually come. No matter how long, and how dark the night, the morning light would most certainly come in due time. How could they have been so sure? Because Almighty God had promised in His Word: *While the earth remains, seed time and harvest, cold and heat, summer and winter,* ***day and night,*** *shall not cease.* The night may have seemed very dark, but brighter times were ahead.

Waiting on the Lord for the day

In waiting upon the Lord to usher in the light, the Psalmist gives us an example to emulate. The context of this 130th Psalm is actually that of a discouraging, difficult, downcast and dark time. The Psalm opens with the Psalmist almost groaning: *Out of the depths I cry to Thee O LORD . . .* The Psalm thus encourages all of God's children who are currently going through dark times to 'wait on the Lord', that is, to look to Him in faith and expectation, for whilst the night of suffering and sorrow may seem long, it will not be for ever. Morning will come, says the Psalmist, but meanwhile, he says, trust in God's Word. That is, trust in the revelation that God has given us of Himself in the Bible. Remember that He is all-wise, all-loving and all-powerful and is actually working all things for the eternal blessing of His people and the eternal glory of His name. Wait upon the Lord then in the time of earthly trial, and continue trusting in God and hoping confidently in His Word. *I wait for the LORD, my soul waits, and in His Word I hope; my soul waits for the LORD more than watchmen for the morning, more than watchmen for the morning.* Psalm 30:5 (b) strikes a similar note to this when it says *Weeping may tarry for the night but joy comes with the morning.*

> O child of God, wait patiently
> When dark thy path may be
> And let thy faith lean trustingly
> On Him Who cares for thee
> And though the clouds hang drearily
> Upon the brow of night
> Yet in the morning joy will come
> And fill thy soul with light

Waiting for the eternal Day

The Psalmist's waiting for the morning light can also be applied in a prophetic, as well as a personal way. When those watchmen waited for the dawn, they would be on the look out for a special star to appear in the sky, namely the 'morning star' - sometimes referred to as the 'dayspring'. The appearance of the morning star in the sky would announce that dawn was imminent.

On the very last page of the Bible, in Revelation 22:16, Jesus says of Himself: *'I am . . . the bright Morning Star.'* A lesser know description of the Lord Jesus then is that of the bright Morning Star. He is the blessed and bright Morning Star, because His appearance in the sky will signal His coming again in power and great glory to usher in the dawn of everlasting day, and the end of all sorrow, sadness, darkness and even death itself. Revelation 22:4 tells us of that Day *Death shall be no more.* Revelation 22:3 tells us of that Day *There shall no more be anything accursed* - for Jesus bore away the curse on Calvary's tree (Galatians 3:13). Revelation 22:5 tells us of that glorious dawn: *night shall be no more; they need no light of lamp or sun, for the Lord God will be their light and they shall reign for ever and ever.*

Watching and waiting: waiting and watching

Christians therefore are a waiting and watching people. We are waiting for the Morning Star to appear in the sky. We are awaiting the glorious return of our Saviour in power and great glory. Jesus is coming again, and His coming will usher in the everlasting Day of perfect righteousness and perfect peace.

Christians of a former generation made more of the Second Coming of Christ than perhaps we do today. That Jesus *is* coming again is plain from the Bible. His coming again challenges the Christian to preach the Gospel urgently while there is still time. The thought of His coming again warms the heart of the Christian like nothing else, for in that Day, all will be eternally well, our redemption will be complete, and our fellowship with our Saviour will be greater than we have ever known before. In Revelation 2:28, God makes the promise to those who are faithful to Him: *I will give Him the Morning Star* - perfect fellowship with the Saviour for all eternity. This being so *My soul waits for the LORD more than watchmen for the morning.*

We are waiting, blessed Saviour
We are watching for the hour
When, in majesty descending
Thou shalt come in mighty power
Then the shadows will be lifted
And the darkness rolled away
And our eyes behold the splendour
Of the glorious crowning Day.

Chapter Twenty-Nine

There's A Door That Is Open,
And You May Go In ...

Having never lived on my own before, the move to my own flat necessitated a few adjustments. I still have to take especial care with the front door. The nightmare scenario would be that of locking myself out at an inconvenient time. Then, on some days, half way through the morning at work the thought crosses my mind: 'Did I lock the door?' It is strange how we cannot always remember the things that we do automatically.

Doors. They are vital to our well being. They let relevant people in, and they keep unwanted people out. Interestingly, the Bible also has its doors:-

1. The door of salvation

In John 10:7, the Lord Jesus states: *I am the door of the sheep.* And in John 10:9 He expands on this by saying: *I am the door; if any one enters by Me, he will be saved, and will go in and out and find pasture.*

Jesus' words are easily understood against their eastern background. In Bible days, sheepfolds had no 'doors', but just a space. This being so, at night, the shepherd himself would lie across the entrance to the sheepfold, effectively becoming its 'door.' Sheep could only enter the safety of the fold 'through' the shepherd, and once inside, it was the shepherd who kept them safe, fending off the wolves and other undesirables out to damage and harm the flock.

The picture of the sheepfold and its shepherd which we have here, is an earthly picture of eternal salvation. It is through Jesus that we enter into eternal life and salvation. *I am the door; if any one enters by Me, he will be **saved**.* It is through Jesus therefore that we are both saved and kept safe. He was to say a few verses later: *I give them* (i.e., 'My sheep') *eternal life, and they shall never perish, and no one shall snatch them out of My hand* (John 10:28).

2. The first door of the Bible

The first mention of a door in the Bible occurs in Genesis 6:16, where God commanded Noah to make an ark. His instructions included this: *and set the **door** of the ark in its side* (Genesis 6:16).

Thousands of years ago, the Bible tells us that God judged the world by a great, universal flood, because its wickedness was so great. There was salvation for Noah and his family in the ark though. The ark enabled them to rise above and escape from God's judgement. So what an illustration of the Lord Jesus Christ is the ark. The waters of judgement could not harm Noah and his family at all. When the waters of judgement came, they were saved and safe behind the ark's door. Genesis 7:16 reads: *and the LORD shut him in.*

3. The door of the Tabernacle

There is a further reference to a significant door in the time of Moses, when the Tabernacle - 'the Tent of Meeting' - was built. God Himself, although everywhere - for He is omnipresent - yet presenced Himself in this special tent in a very special way. Every detail of the Tabernacle speaks of Christ, the Word Who was to become flesh and 'tabernacle' Himself among us in due time.

We notice that there was only one door to the Tabernacle. It had only one entrance, and the first item of furniture which one would meet upon entering was the large altar of burnt offering. Exodus 40:6: *You shall set the altar of burnt offering before the door of the tabernacle of the tent of meeting.* Again, what a picture of Christ we have foreshadowed here. The Bible is clear that there is only one way to God, and that way is through

Jesus. Jesus said: *I am the way and the truth and the life, no one comes to the Father but by Me* (John 14:6). And the only way to God is through the 'altar' of Calvary, where Jesus was sacrificed, shedding His blood for the forgiveness of sins and the reconciliation of sinners to God.

4. The door of opportunity

In Colossians 4:3, Paul makes the specific request: *pray for us also, that God may open to us a door for the Word.* And in Acts 14:27, we read of a happy church gathering which *declared all that God had done with them, and how He had opened a door of faith to the Gentiles.*

Yes, only God can open the door of our hearts and shine His light into them. How humbling that is. If you are a Christian in this non Christian world, give thanks to God for opening your heart and mind to your sin and plight, along with His gracious provision for sin in the Saviour. Also, why not be like Paul, and pray that God, in His grace will open the hearts of your friends to Jesus? Pray that He will give you both the opportunity and the ability to witness gently to the Saviour Whom you love so much. In Revelation 3:8, the risen, ascended, glorified Saviour says to the church at Philadelphia: *Behold, I have set before you an open door, which no one is able to shut...*

4. The door into glory

Finally, in Revelation 4:1,2, we have the most remarkable vision. John records how *After this I looked, and lo, in heaven an open door!* How wonderful to be permitted a peep into glory. What did John see? He saw that *a throne stood in heaven, with One seated on the throne!* And it is good to know that. It is good to know that even in these days - when things seem so dark, difficult and discouraging, and we are tempted to believe that evil is winning - God is still on the throne. *Hallelujah! For the Lord our God the Almighty reigns* (Revelation 19:6).

So there are some of the doors of Scripture. But ending as we began, we recall Jesus' words. He is the door of salvation, for He said: *I am the door; if any one enters by Me, he will be saved* (John 10:9).

> There's a way back to God, from the dark paths of sin
> There's a **door** that is open and you may go in
> At Calvary's cross, is where you begin
> When you come as a sinner to Jesus.

Chapter Thirty

"Let's Say The Grace Together ..."

2 Corinthians 13:14 is one of the most well known and well used verses in all the Bible. In Christian circles it is almost on a par with John 3:16 for fame. 2 Corinthians 13:14 reads *The grace of the Lord Jesus Christ and the love of God and the fellowship of the Holy Spirit be with you all.* The number of public worship services which have been closed using this verse is beyond calculation. The verse though is infinitely more than the ecclesiastical form of a factory hooter, signifying 'All out. It's closing time.'

By way of introduction, we notice that 2 Corinthians 13:14 is Trinitarian. It mentions the Lord Jesus Christ, God - by which it implies God the Father, and the Holy Spirit. As we have already seen, the Trinity is basic to Christian belief about God. To repeat the *Shorter Catechism* again 'There are three persons in the God-head, the Father, the Son and the Holy Ghost and these Three are One God, the Same in substance, equal in power and deity.'

By way of introduction, we also notice that the unique blessing of the Triune God, as enunciated in 2 Corinthians 13:14 is not the privilege of a special elite, but to *all* - that is, to all Christians; those who have realised their need and have sought the grace, love and fellowship of God to meet it.

Let us though unpack this verse a little. If we really know the reality behind it we will be supremely blessed, with a blessing that this world can neither give nor take away.

1. The blessing of the second Person of the Trinity

2 Corinthians 13:14 begins with Paul's desire that all his readers - and by implication all Christians - would know *the grace of the Lord Jesus Christ*. Unusually, in this instance, Paul puts the second person of the Trinity first, changing the usual order of Father, Son and Holy Spirit. The question is, Why? The answer is because faith in Jesus always comes first in the soul's experience of salvation. It is through Jesus that we come to know God, for as 'God in the flesh' Jesus is the unsurpassed revelation of the invisible God. Notice that Jesus is God, for 'Lord' is a title of deity. The description here is a full one. The One Who is God is also the Saviour - for Jesus means 'Saviour' as He is also the promised Messiah. 'Christ' is not so much a name, but a title. It means 'anointed one' or Messiah.

Knowing the 'grace' of this Lord Jesus Christ means knowing His gift - His unmerited, undeserved blessing and favour. It means knowing the salvation which only He can give. *The free gift of God is eternal life in Christ Jesus our Lord* (Romans 6:23). *Every one who believes in Him* (the Lord Jesus Christ) *receives forgiveness of sins through His name (Acts* 10:43). The *grace of the Lord Jesus Christ* therefore takes priority in the Triune blessing we are considering.

> There's a way back to God, from the dark paths of sin
> There's a door that is open, and you may go in
> At Calvary's cross, is where you begin
> When you come as a sinner to Jesus.

2. The blessing of the first Person of the Trinity

Paul's desire is that we also know *the love of God* - the love of God the Father. Here, words fail us, for the love of God, which is the root source of our salvation, is beyond measure or description. In the Bible, God's love is not described in the abstract, but rather it is known by what it does for us. The Bible offers no formal definition of the love of God, but it does describe what the love of God effects: *God so love the world that He gave His only*

Son ... (John 3:16). *God shows His love for us in that while we were yet sinners Christ died for us* (Romans 5:8). *In this is love, not that we loved God but that He loved us and sent His Son to be the propitiation for our sins* (1 John 4:10).

A master theologian wrote the following precise and rich definition of the love of God. It is the nearest that we have come to a definition of that which defies definition:-

'God's love is an exercise of His goodness towards individual sinners whereby, having identified Himself with their welfare, He has given His Son to be their Saviour, and now brings them to know and enjoy Him in covenant relation' (James I. Packer, *Knowing God,* p. 139).

3. The blessing of the third Person of the Trinity

Lastly, we notice that the well known benediction of 2 Corinthians 13:14 expresses the desire that we know personally the blessing of *the fellowship of the Holy Spirit,* that is, the participation in, or communication of, the Holy Spirit, for it is the Holy Spirit Who imparts the love of God and the grace of the Lord Jesus Christ to our hearts, so that we know and enjoy them personally.

A good verse which elucidates *the fellowship of the Holy Spirit* is 2 Thessalonians 2:13, where Paul wrote: *we are bound to give thanks to God always for you, brethren beloved by the Lord, because God chose you from the beginning to be saved, through sanctification by the Spirit and belief in the truth.* As the *Shorter Catechism* states: 'We are made partakers of the redemption purchased by Christ by the effectual application of it to us by His Holy Spirit.

It is the Holy Spirit Who convicts us of our sin and lost plight. And it is the Holy Spirit Who then enables us to trust in the crucified Saviour Who died to save us from our sins. Then, in trusting Christ, we are reconciled to God the Father.

And so we see the Trinitarian nature, not just of God, but of our salvation too. The Father sent the Son, and the Father and the Son send the Holy Spirit. The Holy spirit leads us to Christ, and Christ reconciles us to the Father, to the glory of the Triune Name. No member of the Trinity ever works in isolation. There is a perfect harmony and order in God's salvation. The Triune God effects Triune salvation.

How fitting it is then to end a church service with 2 Corinthians 13:14. Surely, the greatest blessing which any of us can ever know is the blessing of the Triune God - knowing and rejoicing in His grace, love and fellowship. It is customary to add an 'Amen' to the blessing. 'Amen' means 'It is so' or 'May it be so'. May *The grace of the Lord Jesus Christ and the love of God and the fellowship of the Holy Spirit be with you all.* Amen.

SOLI DEO GLORIA